The Fool and His Enemy

THE FOOL
AND
HIS ENEMY

Toward a Metaphysics of Evil

J. R. Nyquist

THE FOOL AND HIS ENEMY:
Toward a Metaphysics of Evil

By J.R. Nyquist

July 2020

ISBN: 9798666501382

Cover design by Rob Buscher, based on a design by Peter Hoffstätter, designer for the German language World October Edition

Front cover photo of George W. Bush and Vladimir Putin by Paul Morse, courtesy of the George W. Bush Presidential Library and Museum / NARA

Interior design by Bravura Books

CONTENTS

THE SPECIFIC POLITICAL distinction to which political actions and motives can be reduced is that between friend and enemy. This provides a definition in the sense of a criterion and not as an exhaustive definition or one indicative of substantial content. Insofar as it is not derived from other criteria, the antithesis of friend and enemy corresponds to the relatively independent criteria of other antithesis: good and evil in the moral sphere, beautiful and ugly in the aesthetic sphere, and so on.

— Carl Schmitt[1]

Chapter 1

The Fool Alone With Himself

A Schizophrenic Prelude

Our objective must be to defend society from its enemies. But who are its enemies? How can a society, which agrees on nothing, whose diversity must be inclusive of everyone, defend itself? Add to this, that our enemies are among those we cannot exclude. It is an extraordinary position to be in, an indefensible position, and quite untenable. We have been systematically led—by our leaders—to deny the existence of our enemies. Denial is seen as a path to peace, and peace is the thing we value more than courage, more than justice, more than our own existence. This is where we have arrived, and it is a very dangerous place to be.

If we say there is no enmity, and believe with all our might, then we reckon war cannot happen. Especially, a nuclear war cannot happen. In this formulation, peace can be achieved by a process of denial. We deny, for example, that Islam has been Europe's enemy for many centuries. We deny the history of the Islamic invasions, and the recent declarations of Muslim clerics. We attribute everything to a handful of terrorists. By this process we eliminate the very reality of enmity itself. We deny that "racism" is also a trait of non-European peoples. We deny that Iran wants nuclear power in order to build a bomb that can be dropped on Europe. We deny that Russia wants her empire back. We deny that China wants to dominate the Pacific.

This game of denial, which we play with ourselves, is a very sly sport. We wouldn't want to make a big public spectacle about all these denials. It is best to use an indirect method, like a protest march in favor of Muslim refugees. The xenophobe and the homophobe are to be rebuked. They live in that fearful negativity which waits on enemies, which believes in enemies. Yes, we are opposed to that way of life now. Our gospel is the brotherhood

1

of man, of course. There need be no enmity, no conflict. We are inclusive, and if anyone is not included, then we are the ones at fault. We are the ones who have caused those poor Muslim boys to crash passenger planes into the World Trade Center and the Pentagon. Such is our catechism. Such is our Holy Grail.

In this business we ought to be circumspect, however. We ought to whisper our catechism so as not to disturb the reactionaries and throwbacks in our midst, of which the present author happens to be one. We must not rile him up, even though his writings are irrelevant since *we* dominate the journalism business and book publishing. *We* determine who goes up and who goes down, which book sells and which author gets positive reviews, with very few exceptions. In the end, we hope the reactionary repents his outrageous opinions, and embraces Islam or Marxism. It does not matter which golden calf the supplicant bows down to, so long as he doesn't name his country's enemy. Then we might allow him a place at our table. But until then, one cannot easily forgive the reactionary his crimes—which include the first sentence of this book: "Our objective must be to defend society from its enemies."

We cannot have enemies. We have eliminated all enemies by including everyone in our commonwealth. We are too healthy, too compassionate and spiritually advanced for enmity. We do not exclude people from our society. Imagine how absurd it would be to exile the Arabs, the blacks, the Hindus and the Muslims. It is unthinkable that we should be one thing and they should be another. We are all one! In the public square, where instinctive animals yet graze, let us whisper our catechism. We will affirm our new global religion so as not to disturb the ape-men clinging to the last vestiges of their Western heritage. We do not want them to become enraged or violent. We want them to remain asleep, and passive, so that our advance can continue unobstructed. The present author is a man of despicable obsolete ideas. Why bring him into the discussion at all? He really is nobody. So let him remain nobody. His concerns are not our concerns. Tolerance and inclusivity do not apply to him. His point-of-view is a scandal. Everything old is scandalous, and everything that is old is obsolete. The word enemy—what does that mean? It unmasks the author as a homophobe, sexist and racist. What else is signified when an author writes, "Our objective must be to defend society from its enemies"?

What enemy would he dare to name? We look around and see good people, poor people, black people, Mexican people, Asian people, Muslim people. We look in the mirror and there we find the best people of all—pure and noble and optimistic about the future of mankind. We see no necessity for wars or weapons—especially atomic weapons. Surely, we have taken great pains to cultivate our innocence when it comes to wars and warmongering. Quite naturally, we shake our heads at the CIA and Pentagon, even though we have controlled these agencies for many years. We shake our heads at the U.S. nuclear arsenal, even when our president—Mr. Barack Obama—is the man with his finger on the nuclear button. We know he won't push that button. Can we say the same thing about someone who writes, "Our objective must be to defend society from its enemies"?

We are moving in the right direction. We are taking it slow and removing one regiment from the Army at a time, one ship from the Navy at a time, one squadron from the Air Force at a time. Once our program of all-inclusivity is completed, we will establish the brotherhood of man and the sisterhood of woman and the personhood of the transgendered. The bourgeois family will be a thing of the past. Marriage will not exist, except homosexual marriage. Every man will be the father of every child, and every woman will be liberated from motherhood. No nations will remain, but only citizens of the world. Then our paradise will be finally established on earth and the hatred of man by man will be a thing of the past. The author of this book will then be locked away in a madhouse, muttering to himself, "Our objective must be to defend society from its enemies."

What a horrible idea! The author should cease and desist. We turn the page against him. We insert our text over his. He presses forward and fights to hold the page by asking, "Shall we defend or not? Shall we survive or not? Shall we think of our posterity or not?" We meet his questions with silence and contempt. Those endowed by endowments, and funded by fundaments, will turn their backs upon him. Free trade will bind the world together, say the capitalists. The brotherhood of man is an evolutionary certainty, say the biologists. The integration of the First and Third Worlds is a necessity, say the bureaucrats. We must stop man-made global warming, say the climate scientists.* But the author does not believe in free trade, the brotherhood of man, the integration of tribes and peoples or man-made global warming. He says, in response to these progressive pillars, that *we* are insane, that *we* belong in a madhouse. The arrogance and ignorance of this author knows no bounds. He proposes the inversion of everything we believe to be true when he says, "Our objective must be to defend society from its enemies."

Which society would he have us defend? Now there, the joke is on him. Undoubtedly it must be the same society that once held Africans as slaves. Undoubtedly it must be the same society that let robber-barons rob and husbands oppress wives. This author, this throwback, would have us pledge allegiance to the "Flag of the United States of America, and to the Republic for

---

* Most climate scientists *do not* endorse the man-made global warning thesis. See the original 8 March 2007 British Channel 4 documentary, *The Great Global Warming Swindle.* Here you will watch a parade of the best climate scientists debunking anthropogenic global warming theory, calling it "propaganda."

which it stands, one Nation, under God, indivisible, with liberty and justice for all." Who could utter that pledge with a straight face? A further scandal, if truth be told, is the author's respect for Aristotle. This is the same Greek philosopher who taught that some men are superior to others, and by nature deserve to rule over "women, slaves and barbarians." Who believes in that sort of thing anymore? Who pledges allegiance? Does anyone take an oath without breaking it? National loyalty must be some kind of joke, and those who believe in such things, well, they are like dinosaurs. Their exploitive, backward, white, capitalist republicanism ought to be eradicated. We are far too enlightened, and vigilant, and aware of the many crimes committed by European man to be suckered into his defense. This crazy author, this war-monger, must be put down; for he insists that "Our objective must be to defend society from its enemies."

Shall we, then, discuss the absurdity of this idea? Of course, in order to defend this republic of his, he must postulate enemies. After all, he likes nuclear weapons. He likes the idea of a nuclear war. Our strategy must be, and should be, to ignore him. Set him in the wilderness to orate over cacti. Then only the reptiles of the desert will hear the empty sound of his voice. It is enough that there are discordant voices in our cities—especially on the radio—who stir up the instincts of the ape-men. But these will soon pass away. Oh yes, *we*'re in control and there's nothing these old dinosaurs can do about it. In fact, these same old capitalist reptiles are moving to the Left day by day; for we have been working on them, and colorizing them with a barely discernible pink brush. Yes, even the "patriots" and gun enthusiasts will be made to kiss the Muslim and the homosexual in the end. They will embrace political correctness—and if not, they will succumb to old age and death. In the last analysis what shall remain of their "lost world"? Sexism, racism and classism will be gone. *We* have fashioned the new generation. *We* educated them. *We* entertained them. We tell them what to think. *We* have even trans-formed Christianity.* The ancient wisdom will have been transmuted into our ideology. We will, by an irrevocable process, dictate the ideas of the future. We will remake society in our image—according to our all-wise prescrip-tion. And it will be accomplished through a process of elimination. Do not the occultists teach that the elimination of an idea signifies the elimination of its corresponding reality? Think, then, of the great service we have done mankind! If you worry about getting cancer then you will be diagnosed with cancer. If you think you have enemies, then you will have enemies and war will follow and the world will become a radioactive wasteland. To make mat-

---

* See Rama Coomaraswamy's *The Destruction of the Christian Tradition* (Bloomington, Indi-ana: World Wisdom, Inc. 2006), p. 1, where the author says, "Vatican II can be described as a turning point in the history of the Catholic Church."

ters worse, it will be your own fault! And there is much more to this. We have to destroy the European's sense of superiority. Let the Muslims come. Let the Asian and the African have dominion. Let their flash-mobs sack our stores and rape our women. (We weren't having babies with them anyway!) The ideal of harmony which we now pursue requires the eradication of the greatest evil of all history—which is European civilization. Let us bow our heads in shame and issue a string of apologies to the other tribes of the earth, to the women of our species and those exploited millions who are daily trampled by the corporate greed of the bourgeoisie. By our policy we kill many birds with one stone. We destroy what must be destroyed, and none will stand in our way. Evil itself has been abolished. All enemies evaporate before our magic incantation. This silly author, this warmonger, is now thoroughly discredited by the first sentence of this book: "Our objective must be to defend society from its enemies."

Enemies belong to the past, as do dinosaurs writing books about the threat from Russia and Islam. Such people would vindicate Joseph McCarthy if they could, or "save Western civilization." To hell with Western civilization—let it die! For that is what is happening already. We are slowly killing it, and do not object if an opportunity for a quicker death comes along. (After all, we do not have unlimited patience.) The process is slow and works by inches: generation by generation, little by little. Our method is not widely discussed but certainly well-known to the faithful few (i.e., the leading activists of the Party). We control the schools and the universities. We are molding the consciousness of the next generation. In twenty years we will have eradicated the difference between man and woman, between black and white, between rich and poor. We will have our victory, and after this victory the old world and its doctrines will be gone: property rights, gun ownership and nuclear weapons—all of them, eradicated. The ape-men who hold onto these vile relics will be old and worn out, their children will replace them, filled with *our* ideas, *our* principles, and *our* inclusiveness. We shall then invite the world to dinner. We shall let them camp on our lawns, in our gardens. The whole Third World will come to America and Germany. We will throw a block party for them. Then we shall have a new world, a happy world, based on love and charity. The author of this book fears that our concept of global harmony is a one-way harmony, that our tolerance is a one-way tolerance. Ha! So what! Western civilization has to go and must dissolve itself—out of philanthropic necessity—if only to reinvigorate the fallen confidence of backward peoples; if only to ensure a golden age of peace. Of course, we shall eradicate the very idea of "backward peoples." Who is to say that the West is not "backward," with its moon landings and massive food production, computerization, modern infrastructure, hospitals, cars and jet aircraft?

The Fool and His Enemy

Who dares to suggest that a grass hut in the midst of the Congo isn't the envy of the world? Who is to say, for that matter, that the Muslim fanatic, awaiting the Twelfth Imam, is not correct in his theology? Let us dispense with the language of humiliation which postulates more advanced and less advanced peoples, true or false religions, right or wrong ideologies. The only religion we need fear is Christianity of the older type. Therefore, we have taken the churches in hand. We are fixing them. These churches will help put this crazy author in his place. A reconfigured Christianity will contradict anyone who dares to write, "Our objective must be to defend society against its enemies."

We are the ones in control now and ***our*** objective has nothing to do with defending society because *we are the enemy of that self-same society*; and now, at long last, we can level this civilization and remake it in our image, according to our likeness.

The Author, On Recovery of His Own Voice

The preceding paragraphs were written to demonstrate that there is a voice in our midst; a propaganda, a social poisoning, which is so subtle, so deep and thoroughgoing, that we cannot always distinguish it from our own true thoughts. It is, as it were, a false conscience and imposition from outside the self. This false conscience is a revolutionary weapon designed by men who seek power over others. Theirs is an attempt to hijack the human race by taking over education, the media and government. This takeover began gradually, incrementally, many years ago. Those who began it are now in their graves, but the ideas and political movements they left behind have a significant degree of control over society's core institutions today. One might say that they have constructed a kind of cultural leveling machine that is clearing a path to a new and untenable secular order.

What can we say about this untenable order? As early as 1927, Carl Schmitt suggested that "all significant concepts of the theory of the modern state are secularized theological concepts." This is significant insofar as the omnipotence of God has been transposed onto the State. Year by year the State acquires more power, more responsibility. It substitutes the political for the spiritual. It wipes away the old moral law, replacing it with a new political morality. Here, politics swallows up everything. Here, every sphere of activity becomes a battlefield on which everything is leveled to make way for the "world to come." Man's salvation is now a political question instead of a religious question. Here is a theme that lies at the back of *everything*—a theme which has been planted, like a serpent's egg, inside the intellect of modern European man. And there, deep within, it has hatched, it has grown. And now it whispers from deep inside of us—a false voice and suicidal conscience that redirects all thought, and all actions.

Before there can be an exorcism of this inward demon, before the false voice of the inner snake can be cast out, a terrible reckoning must occur. By writing these words *prior to that reckoning*, it is perfectly obvious that almost no one will understand; for the false inner voice is now dominant. But once the reckoning begins, the scales will fall from men's eyes. And so, these words, so pointless at the time of their writing, may yet be worth something *after the fact*. The real battle, deep underneath the surface, is a struggle for man's soul—an undefended frontier.

Napoleon once said, "The moral is to the physical as three is to one." Without question, the moral sphere belongs to the soul. By assaulting the soul of man, civilization's enemy has turned our flank. The subversion of the whole has taken place through spiritual and intellectual attacks, which are disguised behind the mask of various diversionary "ideals": (1) the desire for "social justice"; (2) global warming; (3) world peace; (4) and universal prosperity. When we hear such subjects bandied about, we must not be taken in. These items have no spiritual significance whatsoever. Each is a fool's errand.

For those who do not believe in the soul, this attack has been doubly catastrophic because its effectiveness is magnified by the vacuum of unbelief. Those who have abandoned spiritual things for fool's errands have lost the battle before it has begun. They have given up the high ground. They have assured the demoralization of civilization; for the soul harbors those eternal concepts of man and woman, morality and divinity, which are most essential for the healthy continuance of ordered human life.

The perpetrators of this assault are, at bottom, nihilists. They favor destruction, perhaps unconsciously, for its own sake. There is no rational reason to credit these people's assurances that they are fighting for a better world. More than likely, when the smoke clears after their revolution, they will dance jubilantly on top of the rubble. There is every reason to suspect that their grandiose fantasies about "making history" derive from a psychological deficit. The pursuit of power somehow soothes their inner emptiness.

These revolutionaries and nihilists are builders of a new political religion. It is largely due to their manic efforts, together with the work of fellow-traveling reformers and witless philanthropists, that civilization lost its way. The process began to accelerate during the Revolution of 1848. It accelerated again after 1917. European man confused democracy with freedom and equality with morality. Ever since that time we have passed from crisis to crisis. The abandonment of ancient principles, the destabilization of society at the level of the soul, can never be corrected through a process of "progressive" emancipation or reform; for ours has become an emancipation that negates the best men, ignores the best thoughts, and disrespects the most sacred possessions of humanity.

What was emancipated in 1848? What was liberated in 1917? Breaking the connective tissue between the generations of European man was not merely foolish, but suicidal in the extreme. It was Henry Adams who likened the situation to that of a runaway train. Civilization is going faster and faster down the track, without brakes, without any way of stopping. The train must eventually jump the track and smash up. The flavor of madness in all this stems from the fact that those who imagine they are driving the train don't actually know where they are going. What they have in mind, or talk about in public, is a place that doesn't exist—a place that cannot possibly exist (*i.e.*, Utopia). Theirs is a political formula which guarantees that we cannot continue much longer *as we are*; for the train is insensibly accelerating toward some fatal event—like the events of 1914, 1917, 1933 and 1939.

Despite what you have heard about the fall of communism, history did not come to an end on Christmas Day 1991. It continues on its ever-tragic course. This sad and beautiful world of ours is not a child's playground. It is a graveyard of fallen civilizations, of empires invaded and overrun, of elites overthrown and tribes exterminated.

In 1914 the First World War began. It damaged beyond repair the last vestiges of the old civilization. It ended as tragically as it began, with the Armistice of 11 November 1918. The democratic nations imposed a cruel peace on the defeated Germans. Victory was used, at that time, to effect a democratic revolution; that is, to complete the disintegrative work of 1848. At the same time, communist revolution sought entry from the east. What followed was the fiasco of the Weimar Republic, the appearance of National Socialism, the tense situation arising from Europe's entanglement in the wreckage of the Versailles Treaty. A Second World War was in the making—more destructive and tragic than the first.

In light of all this, what did the Allied victory of 1918 signify? What were the consequences of disarming and humiliating Germany? A Second World War was sure to come; and in that war the Germans overran Poland, Norway, the Low Countries and France. The Allies were then on the receiving end of defeat. The meanness of the "democracies," their want of nobility, led them to abandon the four Cardinal Virtues at Versailles in 1919—so that Temperance gave way to greed, Justice gave way to spite, Prudence gave way to ideological arrogance, Courage gave way to the guilty cowardice of appeasement—which led to Munich and the Polish Corridor crisis, with Allied delegations dispatched to Moscow and, in August 1939, to those same Allied delegations sent home when Stalin agreed to align himself with Hitler!

The "democracies" in 1919 were not virtuous. This is one of the defects of popular government, as shown in Thucydides' history of Athens during the Peloponnesian War, especially in his account of "the Melian Dialogue." The democracy in Athens was ruthless toward its enemies, even when ruthlessness was far from necessary. Students of the French Revolution should recall the Terror, the guillotine, the dreadful leveling and violence of mob rule, prettifying itself with slogans of equality and fraternity. There is, in addition, the short-sightedness of the plutocrats whose money greases the political wheels of democracy—and even greases the wheel of socialism. It can be shown that democracies typically confuse virtue with indiscriminate philanthropy—a thing not virtuous but vicious. Under democracy there is a tendency to moral cowardice in the face of popular misconceptions, injustice toward great men, imprudence owing to intellectual mediocrity, and intemperate profligacy in public spending. The whole system tends, over time, toward a demagogic sentimentality, envy of the good—with the greatest care taken for the sake of superficial appearances. After 1848 these effects were multiplied in all European societies—but more so in France and the United Kingdom. These were the nations whose leaders bore the greatest share of blame for imposing the unjust peace of 1919. And here is a lesson, if ever there was one: —Surely, victory is sweet. But only the wise can use victory wisely. Our history of 1914 to 1945 demonstrates that a victorious fool is no better off than his defeated enemy. Oh yes, a victor will enjoy advantages. But the victorious moment passes, and what then? Always it is the victor who is deceived; especially, in the case of the First World War, especially on the matter of his superiority; yet finally, he is deceived about the permanence of his victory.

As man is a spiritual being, and spirit exists outside the realm of conquest, nothing and no one is ever finally or definitively defeated. No enemy is ever completely annihilated. Even the city of Carthage, eradicated in 146 B.C., later vanquished Rome in the person of Septimius Severus, a man who was born in Africa of a Punic father, raised in the Punic tongue, whose thinking was Punic and whose dynasty was fatal. Explaining the character of Severus, Gibbon wrote: "[Severus] promised only to betray, he flattered only to ruin; and however he might occasionally bind himself by oaths and treaties, his conscience, always obsequious to his interests, always released him from the inconvenient obligation."[2] After the usurpation of Severus and the legacy of his dreadful family came the "barracks emperors" and the perpetual anarchy of civil war. Except for a brief revival, the empire fell into oriental despotism, descending thereafter into degradation and corruption.

Thus history, forever until the end of time, is cast in this same mold. That which is triumphant today is laid low tomorrow. If a son of Carthage can become an emperor of Rome, shall England next be ruled by the son of a black African colonial? But no, that has already been the fate of America. And is not America greater than Britain? What is victory if not the carrier of a fatal conceit; that is, a false sense of invincibility?

This son of a black African colonial, this "44th President of the United States," in his 2016 State of the Union Address, declared that the United States "is the most powerful nation on Earth." He explained that U.S. military spending is higher than "the next eight nations combined." He failed to admit, however, that the U.S. military budget consists largely of bloated salaries, fat pensions, welfare subsidies for veterans and expensive medical care. He also did not explain that the Chinese and Russian military budgets do not include such items. The self-flattering and self-congratulating conceit of the victor is always poisonous, always oblivious to reality. "Our troops are the finest fighting force in the history of the world," said this son of a black British colonial. "No nation attacks us directly, or our allies, because they know that's the path to ruin."

Under a regime of braggadocio, with financial bankruptcy looming on the horizon, what must we now think of the West's "victory" in the Cold War? Francis Fukuyama notwithstanding, is this not the greatest self-deception of all? Has this not produced the greatest conceit, the greatest error, in the history of politics? Here we have arrived at last, at the brink of an abyss. Yes, an abyss! For the nations of Europe must decide whether to live or die. At this moment it is by no means certain that they will choose life. *It is by no means certain that they will defend themselves.*

Long ago the aristocratic and priestly orders defended society against foreign armies and subversive ideas. They defended Europe from the Mongols, the Muslims, and the *Albigensian heretics*. But now, who defends Europe? What is defended, at bottom, is a policy of German suicide and Swedish suicide and Dutch suicide, etc. At the time of this writing, it is by no means certain that the nations of Europe will defend themselves; for there is no element dedicated to defense, unless it is the defense of the "environment" or a defense of "animal rights" or "Muslims."

The decline of the clergy and the aristocracy, in the nineteenth century, destabilized the ordered life of Europe as well as the spiritual structure of the European soul. Democracy and freedom were left to sort things out, together with the "invisible hand" of the free market. This was all very naïve, of course, because man requires higher guidance. He requires rank order. He needs structure. The universe was brought into existence by *supernatural mind*, whether we acknowledge this or not. Looking at the commonly held cosmological view of today, which is based on an untenable Darwinism—what *supernatural mind* do we look up to? We look only to monkey-like ancestors born out of a cosmic accident. There is nothing transcendent, nothing higher, no teleology, no metaphysics, no *meaning*! Our ontology is nihilism, our metaphysics denies spiritual reality.

What manner of defense will we now make against the Muslim, who now comes to Europe to build his Caliphate on the bones of our ancestors? If we believe in nothing, if we look to nothing, how will we defend against those who believe in Allah? How far, indeed, have we strayed from our ancient principles, the spiritual precepts of our forefathers? Look how far from nature and instinct and spiritual intuitions and the *Metaphysics* of Aristotle we have come; and now, having moved far beyond the *Politics* of Aristotle, our false idea of humanity leads us to embrace our own destruction—as a needful thing!

This is what progress now signifies; that is, *European suicide.* This suicide has gone by a variety of names. Once upon a time we called it "the revolution," then we called it a woman's "right to choose," or tolerance for the "religion of peace," or "global warming." Each episode here, each transgression against the intellect, each transgression against the spirit, each political trumpet-call, is a gaping and self-inflicted wound upon European man. Just as Polybius wrote about the sudden "dearth of children" in ancient Greece, we may write about the sudden "dearth of children" in modern-day Europe. We should remember, in this context, that the ancient Greeks disappeared altogether. Gustave Le Bon tells us that the modern Greeks are not descended from the ancient Greeks. If this is true, it should serve as a warning to us—a warning to those who believe in homosexuality and feminism and the precepts of Epicurus.

If our thinking is confused, if our instincts are gone, then what will happen to us? As Gustave Le Bon warned in his writings on crowd psychology, "The philosophic absurdity that often marks general beliefs has never been an obstacle to their triumph.... In consequence, the evident weakness of the socialist beliefs of today will not prevent their triumph among the masses."[3] Socialism, feminism, democracy, philanthropy, equality—all these are symptoms of an inward unraveling. All these are tied to a belief in something called "progress." But history does not come with a guarantee of progress. In the second century B.C. Polybius wrote of "the ancients" who taught that the earth had been populated and depopulated many times, that great civilizations had risen and fallen. He claimed that cyclical catastrophes had overwhelmed mankind in the past, leaving only a few human beings alive, who then struggled to repopulate the world. If this is true, what does the doctrine of progress then signify? Humans are limited creatures. We are not heaven-spanning gods.

The great dream of our time, the advent of a socialist millennium, is the most deluded fantasy in the history of man. The religious teachers of old, in their wisdom, knew that we were mortals and not gods. They knew better than to embrace vain ideas about the future prospects of the human race. In the Book of Genesis we find the story of the "Tower of Babel," when a united humanity attempted to build a city with a tower reaching to heaven. "And the Lord said, Behold, the people is one, and they have all one language; and this they begin to do; and now nothing will be restrained from them, which they have imagined to do."[4]

The construction of a universal socialist commonwealth is, in itself, a Tower of Babel. All our globalists, our internationalists, our believers in the "brotherhood of man" are the builders of this same tower. The Bible offers a profound commentary on such projects; and also, an insight into the perspective of those beings—like God—who stand above humanity looking down. Here is a monument to man's overreaching ambition. Here is the grand temple of a secular priesthood, signifying man's propensity to behave without restraint—to do things which are harmful, or ridiculous, or in opposition to the ordering will of Providence. We are so deluded today by our technological victories, that we think ourselves wise enough, and gifted enough, to alter the genetic makeup of food crops. There are even proposals to redesign human beings through genetic science.

The fact that we are not moving heaven and earth to curtail such experimentation, and outlaw all tinkering with plants and animals (let alone human beings), shows that we are without spiritual insight or deeper understanding. We court our own destruction when we exchange the role of "creature" for that of "creator of creatures." For this latter task, we are eminently unqualified. To create a new kind of intelligent being would be an act of such irreverence and cruelty, and would result in such horrors, and such violation of our own spirit as to represent an absolute breach of faith with our own creator. Mary Shelley was very wise, and saw to the bottom of it, when she penned her famous novel on Dr. Frankenstein. To not know one's place, and not know one's limitations, is dangerous on so many levels. For mortals to assume a godlike role over a new set of creatures—artificially made and conceived by technicians—would signify the onset of an unprecedented calamity. A spiritual darkness would cover us, with unimagined evils waiting on the other side of this hellish Rubicon.

In all of this, once again, it is victory that fills us with false hope and self-conceit. We see man's victory in technology, and also in his modern-day wealth. There is the victory represented by our freedom. How quickly we take all of this for granted and forget those teachings, and mock those virtues, which made all these victories possible in the first place. It is fair to say, to some extent, that we have nearly lost the power of self-restraint (relating back to the Tower of Babel story). What will we *not* do? What will we *not* attempt? Certainly, the virtue of Temperance requires that we acknowledge those dark urges which must be restrained if we are to avoid self-destruction. But Temperance has everywhere fallen into disrepute; and prudence is now relegated to the sphere of "prudes." Oh yes, there is a false voice inside of us. Dangerous ideas have been planted—knowingly false and wicked. We must acknowledge that the dangerous voice is something that pre-exists present-day political formations and hidden party structures. Those that would murder a man in cold blood, might also murder humanity by planting an evil thought (disguising it as the answer to various longstanding problems). Yet there is, in all of this, a political component best summarized by the testimony of a former Romanian intelligence chief, Ion Mihai Pacepa, who explained, "During the Cold War, more people in the Soviet bloc worked for the *disinformation* machinery than for the Soviet army and defense industry put together."[5]

To understand this statement, in its historical context, is not easy.

Chapter 2

WHO BENEFITS?

Cui bono: a principle that probable responsibility for an act or event lies with one having something to gain.

— Merriam-Webster.com

Depriving Us of an Enemy[6]

In December 1988 a Kremlin advisor named Georgi Arbatov went to the University of California at Irvine, a place not far from Disneyland. For many years Arbatov had labored in the academic workshops of the Institute of the USA and Canada of the Soviet Academy of Sciences.[7] It was where the favored intellectual playthings of the American left were manufactured. Arbatov had something very special for his American hosts. Arriving at Irvine he unpacked his conceptual goodies and sent a shockwave through the assembled American professors. How easy they were. What children! He towered over them, though he was not particularly tall—representing a regime that had murdered millions and was equipped for killing millions more! He shook hands with Professor David Easton[*] and Harry Eckstein,[8] and soon-to-be Estonian presidential candidate Rein Taagepera.[9] The assembled academics were eager to hear Arbatov's presentation. He spoke English, with a Russian accent. He said, "It's historical, it's human. You have to have an enemy. So much was built out of this role of the enemy. Your foreign policy, quite a bit of your economy, even your feelings about your country. To have a really *good*

---

[*] Wikipedia.org, David Easton, https://en.wikipedia.org/wiki/David_Easton. Easton was rated the second most prominent political scientist in America for the period 1960-70. Author J.R. Nyquist was present when Easton told a 1988 graduate seminar that political scientists should have a "social conscience." At this same session he directed Nyquist to study Karl Marx's *Grundrisse der kritik der Politischen Ökonomie* (Outlines of the Critique of Political Economy), and to present a lecture on the subject.

empire, you have to have a really *evil* empire."[10]

Arbatov's talk closely followed a letter he had written the previous year to the *New York Times* in which he explained that Russia had a "secret weapon" which consisted in depriving America of her enemy.[11] Employing an old theme of communist propaganda, Arbatov suggested the Cold War was being artificially kept alive so that Washington could justify "military expenditures that bleed the American economy white" and policies that promised to draw "America into dangerous adventures overseas...." Reagan's policy of opposing the Soviet Union, he intimated, also caused serious disagreements with allies in Europe and Asia, and a loss of influence in neutral countries. Arbatov then asked, "Wouldn't such a policy in the absence of The Enemy put America in the position of an outcast in the international community?"

By way of a trial balloon, if you will, Arbatov was letting his listeners in on a secret. In fact, he was giving them a glimpse of the future—of what was coming. Whether they wanted to or not, the Americans would be obligated to disarm. But more immediate than any physical disarmament, there would occur an ideological disarmament. In a few years this ideological disarmament would hit Africa like a sledgehammer, leading to the replacement of the white South African regime in Pretoria with a black communist regime under Nelson Mandela and the African National Congress (ANC). This, in turn, would have a ripple effect throughout the sub-Saharan region. At the same time, a path would be opened in Latin America along similar lines—a path that Hugo Chávez and Luiz Inácio Lula da Silva would follow. It was only a matter of time before the communists would take power in Venezuela and Brazil, Ecuador and Bolivia. A quiet revolution might even be possible in America, given the unnoticed collapse of anticommunism. It was then, in 1991, that communism was freed from its shackles. In America, loyalty oaths were done away with on many college campuses. In effect, the elimination of the "image" of the Soviet Union as an enemy would be a tremendous step forward for local communists on every side.

Adopting a reasonable pose, and abandoning the outward flourishes of communist dogma, the USSR and its allies throughout the world would destroy anticommunism at a single blow. Here, indeed, was a "secret weapon" for accomplishing a great victory. How this weapon was to remain secret, even as it was being publicly discussed, depended on two points: First, the Americans never understood how flexible communism was; and second, the West would never see that "taking away an enemy" was itself a political maneuver through which the Cold War could continue seamlessly and invisibly. The apparent collapse of communism would be believed and the wrong lessons would be learned. All the while, the core constituency of the new religion would be free to advance to power within various countries—including the United States.

The skills required to accomplish this "maneuver" were carefully cultivated by the top echelons of the Communist Party Soviet Union for many years. Moscow had conducted experiments, and despite the way things spiraled out of control in 1989 and 1991, Moscow's strategists had second and third tier cadres to throw into the battle. These were men of charm, who understood the West, who knew how to make conservative or liberal noises. Georgi Arbatov was such an operative. When Rev. Billy Graham went to Moscow in 1982, Arbatov met and talked with the evangelist for over three hours. Graham, who had previously denounced communism as "Satanic," came out of his meeting with Arbatov and said, "I have met a very wonderful official here."

How wonderful indeed! On that December day in 1988, before the assembled academics of UC Irvine, Arbatov said, "We have to destroy the image of the enemy." It was not a question of actually destroying the Soviet Union or communism. The appearance of destruction was all that mattered. It was entirely a question of stage effects, showmanship, and the elimination of the old brand; that is, the hauling down of the red flag with the hammer and sickle, the renaming of a few cities,* the setting up of KGB-controlled entrepreneurs and billionaires. Voila! Add water and stir—and there it was: capitalist democracy!

To understand the relationship between this overall design and the Kremlin operative, Mr. Arbatov, it is important to remember that he was not a free man. Arbatov was not speaking for himself, and he was not discussing his own personal opinion. He was a messenger sent from Moscow to America. His whole life was spent under the discipline of the Communist Party. At each moment he was carefully weighing his words. These were calculated to serve his Kremlin masters. Furthermore, his talks were not merely descriptive of Soviet strategy—they were part and parcel of that strategy. Here was a link in a messaging system. On one level, Arbatov was entertaining the left-of-center liberals as he baffled the conservatives. On another level, he was passing operational information to local American cadres. These alone would grasp the full significance of what was being said. The others, blind and dumb, could know nothing of the constraints, duties, party discipline, orders and plans which stood behind Arbatov's remarks.

It was inevitable that the West would misunderstand Arbatov, just as they had misunderstood Gorbachev. The media and the political leadership of the West assumed that communism was liberalizing, that Gorbachev had somehow renounced his party's enmity for the capitalist world. Quite naturally, such a renunciation from the communist side required a similar re-

---

* Names can be deceptive, though sometimes they provide clarity. For instance, the administrative district around St. Petersburg is still officially named *Leningradsky Oblast*. The railway station in Moscow that sends trains to St. Petersburg is still *Leningradsky Vokzal*.

nunciation from the free world. The communists were being nice. Why not return the favor? And who would dare to acquire, in this matter, a reputation for bad manners? Therefore, none would denounce Mr. Arbatov as merely "pretending" to set aside Cold War enmity in order to win advantage for the Communist Party Soviet Union. Such a reaction would have been, at the time, socially inappropriate and politically "unthinkable." With all that was being done in those years by Mikhail Gorbachev, there was no room for serious Cold Warriors. Even the mighty pundits of the American "conservative movement," who had led the faithful out of the political wilderness and into the shade of Reagan's "rejuvenating" presidency, refused to suspect Gorbachev of ulterior motives. William F. Buckley would later silence the last of the hardened skeptics when he publicly attacked the former chief of the CIA's counterintelligence staff, the late James Angleton, in the pages of *National Review* (after the August 1991 coup in Moscow). There appeared, in those years, a number of books on Angleton, who had been the Cassandra of the CIA. It was Angleton who warned that an unprecedented Soviet deception was being planned. To clinch his argument, Angleton brought forward a KGB defector named Anatoliy Golitsyn who wrote a detailed book about Soviet deception strategy and the coming fake democratization and liberalization of the Soviet Union.[12] In 1984 Golitsyn predicted that the Communist Party Soviet Union would forfeit its monopoly of power.[*] But, he said, this forfeiture would be a façade. The Party would retain control through its clandestine networks, operatives and the KGB. One would think that Golitsyn, having successfully predicted the rise of a new and liberal Soviet leader, was owed a fair hearing with regard to his predictions of a larger Soviet deception policy—especially from American conservatives. But the intellectual leaders of the conservative movement were not as thoughtful or deep as they pretended. While communism appeared in the open, they opposed it. When it went underground, they forgot all about it. In fact, whenever the communists made liberal capitalist noises, the conservatives were eager to befriend them. For example, when the People's Republic of China appeared to embrace capitalism, and when the Russians later appeared to move in the same direction, the American conservatives behaved in the same way leftists had behaved in the past—becoming fellow travelers and dupes. In this regard America's anticommunists were stuffed with the same dry straw as the leftists, except that they could still talk a good game; but in reality, they were ready to make a deal. It may be said that the entire political spectrum in all Western countries, from Left to Right, was made up of hollow men, as described in T.S. Eliot's poem:

---

[*] i.e., *one year before* Andropov's man, alleged 'reformer' Mikhail Gorbachev, succeeded the deceased Brezhnevite, Konstantin Chernenko, as General Secretary of the CPSU.

We are the hollow men
We are the stuffed men
Leaning together
Headpiece filled with straw. Alas!
Our dried voices, when
We whisper together
Are quiet and meaningless
As wind in dry grass
Or rats' feet over broken glass
In our dry cellar.[13]

Buckley's 1991 attack on Angleton and Golitsyn, together with author Thomas Mangold's allegations that the two men were "clinically paranoid," let all dissenters know what they could expect if they obstinately persisted in Cold War thinking. The conservatives wanted to declare themselves the winners of the Cold War. Quite naturally, the Left was perfectly willing to accommodate this conceit. After all, President Ronald Reagan was now the friend of Mikhail Gorbachev. The anticommunist president had publicly approved an attitude of trust toward the Soviet Union. He called it "trust but verify." This formula was asinine, since every act of Soviet cheating or noncompliance was sure to be covered up later out of sheer political embarrassment. In this matter a politician, once committed to trusting Moscow, could never admit that he'd been duped. Therefore, despite massive cheating from the Russian side on every conceivable arms accord in the period 1991-2016, our politicians remained silent because they were all compromised by their own prior acquiescence and stupidity.

Here we get to the root of the problem. One must never deal with totalitarian functionaries, gangsters, or criminals. Such people can never represent a legitimate state. Becoming a "partner" of such people can only make you an accessory after the fact. It compromises your integrity. Such an association may also lead to spiritual destruction, in the deepest possible sense. Yet the leaders of today's legitimate states always seem ready to become "partners" with totalitarian criminals. At the same time, those who are compromised by relationships with communist or post-communist leaders are obligated to attack men of the highest moral standing—those who tell the truth about totalitarianism.

When big business stands to profit by making deals with China, and pundits lose their syndicated columns because they write honestly about the evils of the Chinese Communist Party, then you know that our political culture is being corrupted. Those who contribute to this corruption are accessories to murder and treason—to all the crimes associated with communism. If any form of a free and civilized society is to survive, those who have adapted their writings to accommodate totalitarianism deserve literary oblivion and will most assuredly be cursed by posterity. Such are empty, lacking real character and feeling.

How does one open a dialogue with a mass murderer? What exactly do you say? And the murderer's henchmen, deputies, successors and admirers—how are we to regard *them*? The answer to this question depends on how we regard ourselves. Where do we stand? Who are our friends and who are our enemies? In December 1988 the professors of UC Irvine adopted an attitude of friendliness toward Moscow's representative. They found Arbatov's approach "refreshing." Arbatov had told them, "We have to destroy the image of the enemy."[14] And the image of the enemy was destroyed—with a simple incantation. The *Los Angeles Times* reported that Arbatov's message "was peppered with good-natured reminders of the sins of both nations" and "echoed the tone of Gorbachev's address … in New York City last week." The Soviet leader and Communist Party General Secretary had promised to cut the Soviet armed forces by 500,000 troops. He promised to scrap 10,000 tanks. He would continue the military withdrawal from Afghanistan.[15]

The believers were many. The doubters were few. "Science is basically a humanitarian cause," Arbatov told the Irvine professors. "Professionals of a similar persuasion are not divided by nations."—But men have always been divided, and always will be divided. Yet the communist builds his new lie, step by step. The old lie, no longer serviceable, is left in the dust. The hollow men, who are stuffed with dry straw, hang on Arbatov's every word: "For many years we thought the world was split into two hostile camps, and the struggle between these camps, socialist and capitalist, would determine the outcome of history. But we have changed a lot of perceptions…. The world is a fragile entity with a web of interdependence; you have to take into account everybody's interests. What is important now is not the balance of power, but the balance of interests."[16]

So said the representative of a regime that murdered tens of millions of human beings, that subverted the Orthodox Church in Russia, smashed Russian culture, oppressed and robbed more than 300 million souls—*and his American listeners were charmed.* Billy Graham had said, "I have met a wonderful official here." At the end of his poem, "The Hollow Men," T.S. Eliot wrote the following lines:

> This is the way the world ends
> This is the way the world ends
> This is the way the world ends
> Not with a bang but a whimper.

These straw men make up a people who will no longer defend society from its enemies. One sees, in this, an explanation for the many rapes in Sweden and Germany, for the millions of Muslims pouring into Europe, for America's unwillingness to defend its culture or its border. In South America we find that the defensive structures of the Hemisphere have been torn to shreds and the enemy has come pouring in. The new religion, as the beach-head of two alien civilizations, is pushing forward with terrible determination. Country after country falls—Venezuela, Nicaragua, Ecuador, Bolivia, Brazil—and behold! It is communism running the show from behind the scenes in every instance: in Pretoria, in the Congo, in Angola and through the Sao Paulo Forum and the Workers' Party of Brazil. Suddenly, the uranium mines that supplied the fuel for the first American atomic bombs are supplying the fuel for North Korea's nuclear weapons! Suddenly, the mineral store-house of Africa is aligned with Beijing and Moscow! In Stockholm they are worried about a Russian invasion and there is talk of Sweden joining NATO!

Do we see what has happened? Surely there was a process, a method, which brought all this about. And when we consider the words of Mr. Arbatov, and ask who he was serving, and see what has become of the world— might we ask the question, "*Cui bono?*"

Inside our souls there is a voice—a seductive, subversive voice—which says, "Everyone must be equal, the world must be as one, the gate of entry must be left open because there are no enemies, no reason to fear, no reason to defend, no cause for alarm." It has been saying these things to us, decade after decade. Yet this voice has an origin. Someone generated it. Someone scripted its words.

– "*Cui bono?*"

Think back to Mr. Arbatov, standing before the professors of UC Irvine. He is telling the Americans that he wants to "take away the image of their enemy." Why does he want to do this? The key question behind all questions, the Rosetta Stone of the twenty-first century, with which all actions, all words, may be translated and all hieroglyphs may be deciphered, is….

– "*Cui bono?*"

Millions of Muslims are pouring into Europe, threatening to collapse the indebted welfare states of the continent as Russia deploys two Guards Tank armies. Some experts believe that North Korea is building a super-EMP weapon intended for use against the United States. Meanwhile, the United States military is shrinking from year to year, its ability to operate overseas is gradually being attenuated.

– "*Cui bono?*"

A new religion seeks to destroy existing society. It seeks to destroy Christianity, the family, the individual. It operates to plunder the global economy, to disrupt race relations, to set women against men and children against fathers. The new religion does this as a matter of course. Though it sometimes talks of equality or fairness, it does not benefit all men equally; rather, it destroys and despoils here and there. It is famous for doing so. Yet fewer and fewer people remember the silent millions, the firing squads and terror famines, the assassinations and civil wars by which this evil thing spreads.

The little subversive voice, which has been planted inside your brain, says that you should put this book aside. *Do not read any more of it. The Americans are the focus of evil in the modern world—not Russia. They pretended to put a man on the moon. They attacked their own World Trade Center on 9/11.*—Ask yourself, truly: Who invented these preposterous lies? For what purpose were they invented? Quite obviously, denying the moon landings is meant to discredit the United States. Saying that the CIA or Mossad placed charges inside the World Trade Center on 9/11 suggests that America is the real attacker, the real threat to peace—not the communists and Islamists.

Who profits from these lies?

Think carefully before you spread a dangerous untruth to other people. Think carefully before you join that army of liars and slanderers. Cultivate the virtue of prudence and watchfulness, which belongs to the wise. Then you will understand what comes next. You will not be surprised when you read the *Pravda* headline, "Russia prepares nuclear surprise for NATO."[17] Being wise, you knew the Russians would turn their deception to account. Wasn't that the plan all along? Wasn't that why Georgi Arbatov went to UC Irvine in the first place—the week after Gorbachev went before the United Nations and promised to eliminate 10,000 tanks?

The intended outcome of the plan appears on the printed page, spelled out in a *Pravda* editorial which celebrates Russia's present military superiority: "Having written off Moscow as a serious geopolitical rival, flying on the wings of inaccessible military and technological superiority, Washington drove itself into a trap, from which it does not see a way out even in a medium-term perspective."[18]

Think carefully and ask the right question, while time remains. *Does a poor backward country like Russia attain nuclear superiority over the United States by accident?* Now slowly reread the words spoken by Georgi Arbatov in 1988, when he said: "What is important now is *not the balance of power*, but the balance of interests."[19] Yes, yes, forget the nuclear balance of power. But then, turn the page and there it is, in the mocking words of *Pravda*:

> …Russia overcame the inertia of collapse and started reviving its power, while the West, being lulled by sweet day-dreams of the liberal 'end of history,' castrated its armed forces to the point, when they could be good [only] for leading colonial

wars with weak and technically backward enemies. The balance of forces in Europe has thus changed in Russia's favor.[20]

The headline of this particular piece reads, "Russia takes complete advantage of castrated armed forces of the West." We also read, "The illusion of world supremacy played a cruel joke on Washington." And who fostered the illusion of American world supremacy? What country supposedly quit the business of nuclear competition, the business of communist subversion, the business of the Cold War? But wait, they did not quit after all.

The Americans did not play a trick on Russia. As you can see, it was the other way around. The Americans wanted to believe that the nightmare threat of Mutual Assured Destruction was a thing of the past. The Americans never wanted a conflict with Russia, or with China. The Americans wanted to live in peace. They wanted to enjoy their happy society, their prosperity and their culture of entertainment. "I have met a wonderful official here," said Billy Graham in 1982. "I like Mr. Gorbachev," Said Margaret Thatcher in 1984. "We can do business together."[21]

In her last book,[22] the Russian journalist Anna Politkovskaya asked if the collapse of the Soviet Union was part of a larger plan. She was shot to death in the lift outside her apartment a short while later, having written too many words. Before we can untangle the jumble of events, we must be clear. Who came out on top? Who dominates Latin America today? Is it the Americans or the communists?

When the Soviet Union fell, Moscow's spokesmen convinced the world that Russia was weak and no longer a threat. It wasn't difficult to make the world believe. With a disintegrated army and a post-communist policy, Russia appeared in the guise of a "partner." But deep within the restricted military zones of the Arctic and Siberia, where no foreigners were allowed to travel, and within the underground cities of the Urals,* military preparations continued. The Americans mistakenly believed they'd won the Cold War. Gorbachev's promises had been false. He had not destroyed the 10,000 tanks as promised. By 2014 the tables were turned, and only military experts could see what had happened. These experts lacked the media clout to explain the situation to an oblivious public. As *Pravda* noted, "When the Americans realized that [they were beaten], it was too late."[23]

---

* Yamantau Mountain complex northwest of Magnitogorsk, and the former settlements of Beloretsk-15 and Beloretsk-16 near Mezhgorye, are among several massive underground construction sites in Russia. The Yamantau site tunnel openings dot a 400 square mile area below the surface, riddled with tunnels and structures at a depth greater than 1,000 feet. According to a highly placed source in Washington, U.S. intelligence experts suspect that the secret headquarters of the Russian Strategic Rocket Forces is located at Yamantau, which may also be a center for nuclear missile and/or warhead production in violation of treaty limits. The facility is so deep that U.S. tunneling warheads cannot reach it.

The Fool and His Enemy

Can Western Civilization Be So Stupid?

Is it possible to deceive a great nation? Can hundreds of millions of people be mistaken about historical events? The short answer is, yes. When information is mainly conveyed through a visual medium—like television—and people do not educate themselves by reading books, it is more than possible. It is the way the world now works.

Already the modern technology of mass communications has been misused and society itself has become subject to vast experiments—thanks to the introduction of television. This new form of communication dominates humanity and is far from a blessing when we consider how it has lowered the intellectual level. The ability to generate and put forward various images, most of them misleading or void of real content, has damaged civilization's chances for survival. Once upon a time society judged for itself. But with television the practical man gradually became a television watcher instead of a book reader.

Neil Postman wrote extensively about the transition from a literate culture to a television culture in his book, *Amusing Ourselves to Death*. He said that we live in a post-literate society. The truth be told, we are addicted to television, we are conditioned by television, and molded by television, and receive our worldview from television. The masses are no longer molded by reading newspapers or books, or by sermons from the pulpit. Only a small minority of the population, without voice or influence, is properly informed by in-depth reading. The best that is written, the best that is thought, is no longer at the center of public discourse. Public opinion is the by-product of soundbites born of a suspect journalistic epistemology. The damage done to the higher end of public discourse is staggering. Television gives the viewer an immediate experience that leads him to overestimate his ability to understand complex phenomena. It is not merely that the viewer is misinformed. The viewer is convinced that he knows the truth when he has merely absorbed a carefully edited set of deceptive images.

As one generation replaces another, the old wisdom and knowledge is lost. A single unrepresentative moment, caught on camera, offers even the most sophisticated audience a false version of events by way of a picture that is worth a thousand words. Here the mind seizes on a visual image, draws conclusions without real familiarity and assumes that seeing is the same as knowing. Yet all these images are, in some sense, edited. All knowledge depends on context, and for the television viewer the context is invariably off-camera. If the television journalist presents a false context, or this is implied by the manner of presentation, a television event becomes a lie. But no, not simply a lie; it becomes a deceptive phantasm made out of images, pictures and dramatic gestures.

Television employs visual stimulation and sensation to persuade its audience. Those who get their news from television, and not from serious books, have no real depth of understanding. It naturally follows that they can be tricked into believing things that didn't happen, told by people who were not there. The busy politician is in the same position as the population at large. Everyone relies on television journalists and pundits. These tell us what everything signifies, drawing conclusions and offering analysis. Since television is produced by professionals whose mission is to convince the audience that theirs is a worthwhile presentation, many viewers will succumb to the opinions presented. The more subtle the presentation, the more souls will be won. The journalist is, typically, a leftist acolyte of the new religion. His bias is often presented as common sense or fact. To assure that society continues to move in the "right" (that is to say, Left) direction, today's journalists are mass produced in journalism schools like sausages in a sausage factory. What has been said of sausages may now be said of journalists. If you knew how they were made, you would never buy one.

There are two dangerous aspects when it comes to the content of television: (1) It serves as a subtle indoctrination in self-gratification through commercial advertising and voyeurism; and (2) it serves as a political indoctrination imposed by journalistic "sausages." Of these two dangers, the second is more difficult to discuss; for as the public's thinking shifts evermore to the Left, it shrivels into a caricature of thought. Any honest discussion of society's suicidal course, of its growing addiction to abnormality, proves oddly controversial. What was normal and vital to all previous forms of society is now devalued. Through its dominance of media, the new religion strives to remake society. Mass social conditioning is accomplished through the schools/sausage factories and the communications media. One might say, with spare irony, that *we are all sausages now*. The realities of human nature, instinct, and innate ideas have been systematically denied by a politics that would preempt the validity of thoughts and feelings which, for thousands of years, have been necessary to the survival of human communities throughout the world. Ideas about sexual differences, about foreign peoples as potential enemies, about intermarriage and the maintenance of tradition—all these ancient human values and instincts have been *devalued*. In fact, instinct itself has been declared null and void.

Our new secular religion *is* political. It is a politics which seeks to negate what is essentially human by decrying traditional norms as the erratum of an irrational past. As such, it destroys and levels everything in its path. As the spiritual man knows, politics is void of spiritual remedy and cannot save mankind. Political activity belongs to the sphere of practical wisdom, social prudence, statecraft and war. It does not bring healing to the soul. It is not a source of spiritual inspiration. It represents, In its socialist manifestation, a special kind of maladjustment and non-acceptance of the human condition. Even an ancient pagan would recoil at the grotesqueries of today's secular religion. As a rebellion against everything that exists, it is destructionist. It finds its god-likeness in an annihilating power as opposed to a creative or redemptive power.

In Carl Jung's book *Aeon* we read about the "shadow" of Christianity, a kind of antichrist force which has been building from century to century, ultimately manifesting in the destructive impulses of modern totalitarianism. Here we find, at its core, a denial and rejection of the realities of human nature—overriding this self-same nature and crushing humanity in the process. It is, as James Burnham called it, "the suicide of the West," for the West is afflicted with this disease. The meaning of "The Revolution" in Russia and China (which are Asiatic and not Western) reduces to a campaign for the extirpation of Western society and Western social structures. What was essentially Asiatic, as before, continues its tradition of despotism and state egoism. Here we find no suicide, but a revolt against a superior civilization that is resented and therefore is marked for destruction—if only to remove the stigma of inferiority. It is within the West, therefore, that the process of Jung's enantiodromia* unfolds. This looming crisis, famously noticed in the 1880s by Friedrich Nietzsche, coincides with the dying out of Christianity and the advent of "European nihilism." The advent of this "nihilism," Nietzsche predicted, would lead to the rise of new Caesars and "wars the likes of which the world has never seen." Would Christianity be replaced with something else? The main candidate was ever and always socialism—a kind of Christianity without Christ. Already Darwin had introduced a creation story without a creator; and with the dialectical materialism of Karl Marx we were given an apocalypse without a Second Coming. This new materialist myth, born under the banner of "science," established a secular religion with a fanatical following. *This is a curious thing to have happened.*

The leftist, yet imbued with a residue of Christian ideas, accepts the scientific pretensions of the new religion. If its precepts have been proven unscientific, he nonetheless believes that the needed discoveries and adjustments for scientific validity are yet on their way. Among the many dangers in such a faith is its disconnectedness from the spiritual requirements of human

---

* Enantiodromia, a term used by Carl Jung to suggest that a superabundance of any force must, in time, produce its opposite (or nemesis). It is related to the principle of psychological equilibrium, and the observed tendency of nature to restore something that has fallen out of balance (i.e., in this case, the human mind). The word enantiodromia was probably first coined by Joannes Stobaeus, who was probably inspired to do so by fragments of the pre-Socratic philosopher Heraclitus.

life. There is danger, as well, in its parodying the democratic and egalitarian mania of the French Revolution. Here we find an implied violence *offered to superior men and superior ideas.* Here is a leveling impulse that opens society to a trans-valuation of values and an inversion of rank order. Notice how the most fashionable things of today are taken from below, not above. That which was characteristic of the lowest strata of society is now honored. The prostitute and the pimp, the gangster, the homosexual, the revolutionary psychopath—are now glamorized. The anti-hero upstages the hero. Sordid mediocrities and villains now emerge as leaders of the people. The sickness itself, having taken possession of the intelligentsia, spreads easily through a disoriented populace—like an epidemic. Television does the rest. Corrupted by ideologies of self-loathing and self-negation, the West now appears to embrace its own annihilation. Having lost its ancient faith, an ethic of mass suicide envelops the whole.

Look at the leaders of your country. Are they not suicidal? With high-sounding words they denounce common sense as "racism" or "Islamophobia." For them, the instinct to defend society must be combatted. Only in this way can the brotherhood of man be realized. The propaganda of political correctness mesmerizes the once great nations of the earth. And all the while, these nations are persuaded to let themselves be destroyed by those who have passed through the great sausage factories—the schools and universities.

As these words are written, children on every continent are subjected to a relentless indoctrination. The process begins by turning off the student's brain, forcing him to listen to specific messages which are presented as models of thinking—models of understanding. "Repeat what we tell you," is the message. This is how one "gets through" school, which has become a center for the mass reformatting of the human mind—an educational sausage factory for human sausages.

The idea that we have reached some grand height of culture, that the current generation is the best-informed or best-educated generation of mankind, is one of those conceits that posterity will mock at. In every age the fool believes in his own greatness, but history will find him out. Men who resemble the great figures of the past do not appear in our time because we have placed our collective fate in the hands of large institutions, including big government, big education and big corporations. We have not nurtured the individual man. We have done everything to stunt his development. Whenever a government or corporate bureaucracy elevates a mediocrity, the effect is to lose the advantage of those who are spiritually and intellectually superior. Of course, the best men are well suited to live happily without the recognition of others. They do not need the affirmation of high rank or public honors to know their own worth. The great loser, however, is society itself. When big institutions, run by small men, thoughtlessly trample the spirit of those who are inwardly superior, true speech and right action is preempted. That is quite obviously what has happened today. It is an early symptom of a coming tyranny. It is, as well, a partial explanation as to why we are less and less able to distinguish between true and false, right and wrong.

To be sure, modern man's undoing grows out of a period of great peace and prosperity in Europe and North America which has been filled with unrealistic expectations. Listening to the politicians of the present day, one detects their lack of historical sense when they insist that the next generation must live as well or better than the previous generation. But the politicians are doing everything to assure that this will not happen! It is worth remembering that the prosperity of the latter twentieth century is not typical in the history of man. It has created, in the present generation of Europeans and North Americans, a forgetfulness and attenuation of the survival instinct which is needed at the outset of a crisis. Brought up on television, with its swarming mass of suggestive images, the world of the latter generations has no real point of contact with the old. From this there can be no turning back. We have entered a "brave new world." The insidiousness of the changes were belied by certain outward appearances—an appearance of something more advanced, more modern, more progressive. But society was being hollowed out. It was becoming rotten on the inside. Men were becoming effeminate and women were becoming masculine. A pathological process, encouraged by the new religion, has taken hold.

Society has been deceived by its enemies because our modern culture has made us more vulnerable to deception. Television has contributed to this. Big government has contributed to this. The promotion of mediocre men, who best thrive in large organizations, has also played an obvious role. And finally, the advent of a secular religion—a political religion—places us in the greatest danger of all.

Chapter Three

THE NEW RELIGION

The coming of Antichrist is not just a prophetic prediction—
it is an inexorable psychological law whose existence, though
unknown to the author of the Johannine Epistles, brought
him a sure knowledge of the impending enantiodromia.

— Carl Jung[24]

A new faith has appeared in our midst. It is secular and political. It is materialist and claims to be "scientific." The New Religion denies the reality of spirit. Only matter exists, only solid objects are recognized. The soul—which directs, perceives, animates—is denied. God is denied. Divine order is denied. Immortality and the afterlife are denied. The New Religion opens upon a cold realm of material cause and effect. The idea of something sacred, of something holy, is viewed with the utmost cynicism. Spirit itself is denounced with that same breath of spirit—a breath that denies breath.

The New Religion is against all religion. It subverts the Old Religion—infiltrates, corrupts, poisons, ridicules. At times it pretends to agree with ancient precepts, wearing a mask of conventional morality; but only, in fact, to destroy conventional morality. As a practical matter, the New Religion cannot devour the Old Religion at one sitting. It therefore advances in small steps. It joins in the prayers of the Old Religion, enters into the churches and takes control of seminaries and schools. It wages war on the level of ideas, yet ideas do not interest it. The New Religion does not seek truth. Its leading acolytes seek power. Their subversive war makes use of many causes. These include abortion and sodomy, minority rights, global disarmament and environmentalism; each cause serves as a flanking action against existing structures which must be broken down:—the family, the church, the nation-state, property rights, motherhood, etc.

The New Religion seems, at first, to make "the people" into its God. But who are "the people"? They are everyone and no one: an amorphous abstraction, a mass of shadows on which any thought or intention might be projected, as upon a blank screen. Therefore, "the people" cannot be a god. Yet, the new faith appears to worship them. Of course, one might call this "good tactics": Tell the proletariat they are the future masters of the world. Tell the poor that they should receive, as bounty, the "ill-gotten gains" of the rich. Tell everyone what they want to hear. In this way democracy is subdued and absolute power is secured.

But then, if "the people" are not the God of the New Religion, then who is? In ancient times Julius Caesar aspired to deification. Today, it seems, we have many would-be Caesars. Each one seeks deification through the exercise of bureaucratic power. Whatever madness led Caesar to cross the Rubicon is yet infectious on every side. The new little gods of the hour can be seen scrambling for power and position. They are generally less competent than Caesar, less interesting—especially in portraying themselves as "servants of the people" or "vanguards of the revolution" uplifting the downtrodden. Yet, they are inwardly criminals at heart. Their sense of entitlement keeps pace with their appetites. They believe they are destined to rule, destined to guide humanity. Plagued by a crushing sense of their own smallness, they are drawn to power like moths to flame. They are animated by an arrogance that speaks for "the people." Logically it follows that *their enemies* are also the *enemies of the people*. Thus they are righteous in the midst of their criminality; for if "the people" are the god of politics, how much greater are the leaders of "the people"?

The true acolytes of the New Religion say that their goal is to make "Heaven on Earth." Ask yourself, then, what kind of being makes such a promise? What kind of entity is empowered to bring Heaven on Earth? Is this not a god? A very modest god, perhaps, if we listen to their demurs; but nonetheless arrogant, if we listen to their promises!—For only a god could bring Heaven on Earth. *But these are men*; so we must conclude they are mad: First, to promise what they cannot deliver; second, to demand power and obedience in the course of their repeated failures; and third, to betray their followers by bringing *Hell on Earth*. And yes, this is what they do. Their grand projects always end in disaster. No wonder they are frustrated. No wonder they are angry at the world—angry at the fictional wreckers and saboteurs who are ultimately blamed. It is no wonder the acolytes of the New Religion have long preached the destruction of everything that stands in their way. As it happens, of course, the entire universe stands in their way.

The New Religion is all about destruction. This is its true focus.[*] To bring

---

[*] See Mephistopheles' self-description in Johann Wolfgang von Goethe's Faust (Part I, Study 1): "I am the spirit that denies! And rightly too; for all that doth begin should

Heaven on Earth requires a vast accumulation of power. How else will the final goal be accomplished? And since the universe itself stands in the way of this goal, an unlimited sum of power must be accumulated if only to remove the universe itself. This signifies opposition to the Creator, even if the existence of this Creator is denied. Therefore, in every sphere the New Religion aims at the overthrow of the symbols and ideals of the Old Religion. To accomplish this, the New Religion reverses the moral order by denying that men are responsible for their actions. Blame is shifted from the individual to the universe (i.e., God). The implication could not be clearer: *The Creator of the Universe is to blame. He must be dethroned.*[25] It is logical in this situation that the New Religion aims at a moral reversal. Good must be shown as evil, and evil must be shown as good. Morality must be denounced, step by step. Thus the doctrine of equality has particular significance—not as *equality before God*. Its significance lies in *moral leveling*. To say that one man is good and another evil *denies* the equality of all men. If all men are created equal then all deeds must be equal. If all deeds are equal, then good and evil are invalid concepts. The reason for upholding egalitarianism, therefore, is not so much to eradicate evil by eliminating inequality. The reason is *to eradicate the good*. Once this is accomplished the way is paved for evil. The old morality is swept away by egalitarianism in the first instance. Next, morality is dissected more carefully and shown to be a tool of "class oppression." This is the real significance of today's socialist revolutions, which are supported by three pillars: (1) moral nihilism, (2) metaphysical nihilism and (3) epistemological nihilism. These doctrines are not advanced openly, or explicitly. They are *implicit* and *inherent* in the New Religion, which aims at destruction and negation (of the entire universe, if necessary). In practice, every success of the Revolution entails a significant destruction of wealth and people. In Webster's 1943 *New International Dictionary of the English Language*, Second Edition, we read the following entry on nihilism:

> **Nihilism**—Primarily, the doctrine that no reality exists; more commonly, a doctrine which denies or is taken as denying, any objective or real ground of truth. The doctrine which denies any objective ground of moral principles;—called also **ethical nihilism**.
>
> [Also] The doctrine that conditions in the social organization are so bad as to make destruction desirable for its own sake,

---

rightly to destruction run; 'Twere better then that nothing were begun. Thus everything that you call sin, destruction—in a word, as Evil represent—that is my own, real element." Translation by George Madison Priest: http://www.levity.com/alchemy/faust04.html.

independent of any constructive program or possibility; esp.
the program or doctrine of a Russian party, or succession
of parties, of the 19th and 20th centuries, who proposed
various schemes of revolutionary reform, and who resorted to
terrorism and assassination....[26]

This entry, of course, is an understatement—yet incisive. Few have seen
through the humanitarian veneer of the New Religion to espy its nihilist
essence and destructive aims. With many acolytes this nihilism may be the
unconscious result of neurotic tendencies. However that may be, it is to the
more sinister acolytes of the New Religion that our attention must now turn.
These are the criminal types—the psychopaths and malignant narcissists—
who find in the New Religion an ideal vehicle. Instinctively such people strive
to eliminate the naturally superior men from positions of leadership and responsibility. By superior men, of course, I do not mean the merely talented or
proficient. I mean the *morally* superior. For those who seek universal plunder,
the wise and honorable are the most dangerous of adversaries. Therefore, dis-
crediting uprightness and mocking goodness is imperative for the political
criminal. He must disrupt ordered life at every opportunity. He must weaken
all the barriers set against him, step by step; for his final goal is the establishment of a criminal state. Therefore, the Gospel of the New Religion is perfectly adapted to his needs—based as it is, on envy. The promotion of envy can
be used to drive the superior man from politics. When the Gospel of Envy
prevails, the corridors of power are filled with vain pretenders, shallow climb-
ers and all manner of inferior persons who are grist for the revolutionary mill.
Once society is debased and weakened, the voting public will be incapable
of resisting low characters and con artists. Without the leadership provided
by superior men, the voting public cannot save itself. They fall for the dema-
gogues, the showmen and actors. They are overwhelmed by the raucous antics
of the political clowns.

It is only the best men, the morally superior men, who can save society.
For only those who are redeemed can redeem in kind. The acolytes of the
New Religion sense this, and hate the morally upright and sincere men—the
men of true heart and courage. Therefore, of its many teachings, the Gospel
of Envy is the decisive weapon for making good into evil and evil into good,
thereby defeating the superior men at one blow; for envy is hatred of the
good for the sake of their goodness. In this matter the Gospel of Envy is like
a stepping stone leading from order to disorder, from nature to perversion,
from civilization back to barbarism.

It is not enough, however, to eradicate the good men of today. It is also
necessary to eradicate them from history. Therefore, the New Religion es-

chews the wisdom of the ancients. It despises authentic history. Those who fought for freedom in the past must be demolished in the present. The *noble man* must be exposed as a class oppressor, racist or sexist. From now on history will be used as a weapon of the New Religion against its enemies—even if those enemies have been dead for twenty-five centuries. Historical facts will be replaced with ideologically loaded interpretations based on errors of omission. The Marxist interpretation that all history is class warfare will be vindicated, and all facts inconsistent with this view will be substituted with new "facts" and new "discoveries" about the past which will be, in every sense, more convenient for the present age.

Of course, the New Religion cannot win by only directing its oppressive tactics at the past and present. It must deploy a prophylactic for the future. What, after all, will prevent a great-souled man from appearing within some future generation to wreck the best-laid plans of the New Religion? Those qualities which make for greatness—independence of mind, intellectual integrity, clarity of thought and courage—must be denounced and undermined as anti-social and subversive. What was formerly the basis of all human progress must now be smothered in its cradle. It is best, for this purpose, to cultivate only false virtues—not masculine virtues, not even feminine virtues.

In its general program of education, the New Religion must inculcate self-dishonesty. This must become habitual within the population. Everyone must become, more and more, unacquainted with reality. What is required is a shady and convoluted polemic, suggesting that reality is *not* worthy of our understanding. Consequently, the teachers of the new faith will decry as inauthentic everything that is not candied, that is not chocolate-filled. They would like to deny that Knowledge is bitter. Since the universe failed to satisfy their sweet tooth, they propose to reshape the universe according to an imagined design; that is to say, a design which is imaginary and fictitious. Destruction and perversion being the primary tools of this design, the acolytes of the New Religion must adhere to a grim program of serial decimations; for example, to remove beauty from art; to degrade religion and mock the supernatural; to stunt the intellect by promulgating false doctrines which accord with political expediency; to sterilize the imagination of man; to corrupt public morality and social habits; to plunder the economy and impoverish the citizens; to spread corruption as a means of political colonization; to encourage infanticide; to deny what is male and female; to slander fatherhood and depose the *Patres Conscripti*.[27] These decimations have been ongoing during the last century, and some are currently in process. After each act of decimation some vital aspect of society is gone, some heartstring is broken. When the great and final flood-tide of destruction is unleashed, only a fraction of humanity will remain. Perhaps there will be nothing left of us—so great is the malice which lurks behind the "revolutionary" façade of the New Religion.

The acolytes of the New Religion will not recognize themselves in this description of their faith and its program. At its core, the New Religion insists on its own goodness. It claims to be based on science. It holds out the promise of liberation from the "darkness" of superstition. Emancipation, says the New Religion, is only possible once we are freed from the old moral rules which have been used to enslave the poor, the non-whites and women. Here abortion is touted as the ultimate freeing act; here the barren womb of the lesbian is celebrated; here the perversion of the Man/Boy Love Association is sanctified; and in the end, the destruction of the family by the breaking of the sacred bond between man and woman is upheld as somehow desirable. It is a good thing, say the acolytes of the New Religion. But how can it come to good? Through all this jilting of the natural order, and all these decimations, and all this plundering, may we ask what they honestly expect to happen? What is finally accomplished? Where is the blueprint of the promised paradise where the lion lies down with the lamb? But there is no such blueprint, and there never was.

The acolytes of the new faith have organized themselves into a political power. They have created institutions and ideologies which, even now, are malevolently destroying what was handed down from our ancestors. The destruction extends to a catastrophic falling off of the birth rate and a general demoralization of society through the perversion of common sense. The destruction appears in every field, on every side—but most visibly in the suicidal policies of the State, the degeneration of the family, and the inability of society to preserve itself as it polarizes, atomizes and disintegrates. For the expert observer, there can be no doubt whatsoever that the way has been paved to an Age of Spoliation. Mankind as a whole is suffering from an epidemic of paranoid megalomania. This was observed and commented upon by Carl Jung in *The Undiscovered Self*, a book written more than half a century ago. If we consult the ancients, we find that madness "coming before a fall" is hardly a modern phenomenon. One finds the following cribbed from a fragment of Euripides: "Whom the gods would destroy, they first make mad."[28] It is a process which starts with irreverence and ends in lunacy. The acolytes of the New Religion believe that man can exist without God. Science, of course, is what gives this idea legs. Men began to think they could live without a sacred sense of things once they had invented a new world of objects. Having done this, they began to suspect that God was one of their inventions. It was only natural that men, thinking in this way, began to deny the existence of a Creator, imagining that all the creatures of this world came about through a spontaneous process called "evolution"—a process which none of the evolutionists have ever properly explained.[29] This is readily seen in the fact that no scientist can credibly say how a single-celled organism came into existence from inorganic matter. Where previously they knew nothing of the complexity of such organisms, they are now under no illusions. The thing had to have been the product of some higher intelligence. It could not have appeared on earth spontaneously. The claims of the materialists, therefore, have no scientific grounding. The New Religion has no leg on which to stand. Technology, progress and science were thought to be all-in-all sufficient for explaining everything; yet the more we know, the less we are able to explain. This has not stopped the New Religion, however, which continues to spread. It has become, quite simply, the disease of the educated classes and the disease of the administrators of mankind. These are, in a manner of speaking, taking over God's office—unwittingly, or in the full flush of madness. Their secularism holds God in contempt. This contempt already *is* madness, of course. Yet it begets further madness. Once you embark upon the path of irreverence, there is no coming back. For how would that be possible? These madmen have already turned against the very source of all sanity. The connection with True Mind, once severed, is lost. What remains is the false, the inauthentic, and the self-deceiving.

Notice the collapse of dignity, the ever-expanding childishness of adults, the devaluation of intelligence and goodness. This is how you destroy ten centuries of the most complex and varied civilization the world has ever known, and debunk it as exploitation, racism and sexism. There is a lack of proportional sense at work here. There is an inability to see context. The teachings of the classical world, the religion of Christ, the traditions of nobility and chivalry—all lost, torn down, mocked. And now what comes? The noble lords are replaced with the ignoble bureaucrats. The intelligence of Aristotle and Plato is supplanted by the tautologies of Heidegger and the demonic fury of Karl Marx. The statecraft of Metternich and Bismarck, Pitt the Elder and John Quincy Adams are given up to the inanities of the Eurozone; capitalism is to be plowed under by the wealth transference schemes of the global warming hucksters. The madness increases with no end in sight.

What has always been thought vicious, inferior and perverse is now celebrated and rendered sympathetic—recast as a victim of the superior man who is now the villain of history. The world, seen from the worms-eye-view of the envious, now moves in reverse direction—from the twenty-first century back to the ninth century; from freedom back to servility, from law to lawlessness, from respect for the individual to tribal violence and feudalism. That is where we are headed, even now, step by step, under the tutelage of the New Religion. Its precepts signify destruction and murder, its politics grows out of the mind of the psychopath. These heretics and criminals have escaped the hangman's noose and the Inquisition's fire, storming the high castle of the State (or worming their way in through democracy's back door) with a tribe of desperadoes at their back. What idiots we have today, believing that *these* are the heralds of mankind's future happiness. Their world is but the world as seen through the *will to power*. Without reverence, without sanctity, without respect for anything or anyone, these barbarians have turned civilized life on its head. Examining the careers of socialist politicians, we can trace the bold advance of the Gospel of Envy as it pushes the world into an abyss of depravity. Civilization must not negotiate with this kind of thing. Civilization must not compromise with it. If this is done, civilization will die—as certain as day follows night. The New Religion moves, irrevocably, toward the destruction and degradation of the whole world—from man as man to man as woman; from woman as woman, to woman as man. The New Teaching leads, step by step, to the end of all things, to the bottomless pit, to the seven angels with seven vials of wrath, and the Four Horsemen of the Apocalypse.

Christianity and Judaism offer a profound teaching on human nature. This teaching is accessible to the simple-minded as well as the sophisticated. Here is wisdom *by way of humility*. The New Religion, on the contrary, does not teach humility. Its teaching promotes arrogance and self-satisfaction. The spiritual destruction wrought by the New Religion is far advanced. One may see this on every side. The study of man under the New Religion has reduced the individual to the status of biological robot with *no* free will and *no* soul. This is in keeping with the New Religion's revolt against the very source of all life—of all being. Even if one does not believe in Satan, one must admit that everything here is Satanic. It is a rebellion urged by envy, by lust for power and position. Such a revolt must end very badly, in catastrophe, as vividly drawn by the Poet John Milton in *Paradise Lost*:

> The infernal Serpent; he it was whose guile,
> Stirred up with envy and revenge, deceived
> The mother of mankind, what time his pride
> Had cast him out from Heaven, with all his host
> Of rebel Angels, by whose aid, aspiring
> To set himself in glory above his peers,
> He trusted to have equaled the Most High,
> If he opposed, and, with ambitious aim
> Against the throne and monarchy of God,
> Raised impious war in Heaven and battle proud,
> With vain attempt, Him the Almighty Power
> Hurled headlong flaming from th' ethereal sky
> With hideous ruin and combustion down
> To bottomless perdition, there to dwell

In adamantine chains and penal fire,
Who durst defy th' Omnipotent to arms.
Nine times the space that measures day and night
To mortal man, he, with his horrid crew,
Lay vanquished, rolling in the fiery gulf,
Confounded, though immortal. But his doom
Reserved him to more wrath; for now the thought
Both of lost happiness and lasting pain
Torments him: round he throws his baleful eyes,
That witnessed huge affliction and dismay,
Mixed with obdurate pride and steadfast hate.
At once, as far as Angel's ken, he views
The dismal situation waste and wild,
A Dungeon horrible, on all sides round
As one great Furnace flam'd, yet from those flames
No light, but rather darkness visible....[30]

There is, in this great poem, a matchless depiction of spiritual revolt and its consequences. The rebellion of Satan, who alienated himself from the very root of existence, reflects the same rejection of divine order we see today in the New Religion. As with Satan, there is unhappiness at playing second fiddle to God. There is unwarranted pride. Yet Satan's attempt to overthrow God is futile, and so is the New Religion's Gospel of Envy. The story of Satan, as described by Milton, presents a portrait of self-overestimation and self-worship.

Today's more troubled personalities—the narcissists and the psychopaths—feel that they too are special, entitled, and deserving of the worship of others. Like Milton's fallen angel, they overestimate themselves. Like Satan, they are sorely disappointed when the universe fails to fall down and worship them. For those men and women who think of themselves as gods or goddesses, a lesser existence must be unbearable. To drag out their lives as ordinary human beings must fill them with rage. It is said that narcissists suffer from bouts of depression and anger, self-loathing and self-deception. We see around us a rising tide of this sort of thing, in private and public life. Perhaps, indeed, there is a connection between Satanism and narcissism. On close inspection we may argue that a great world-negating spirit has appeared in our midst, growing from year to year. One sees, as plain as day, that the modern spirit more and more agrees with Satan's statement to Beelzebub (as depicted by Milton):

To do aught good never will be our task,
But ever to do ill our sole delight,

> As being the contrary to His high will
> Whom we resist. If then his providence
> Out of our evil seek to bring forth good,
> Our labor must be to pervert that end,
> And out of good still to find means of evil....[31]

Here is the supreme spirit of negation. Satan has injured himself by attacking God. He does not repent or seek forgiveness. His perverted obstinacy leads him to Hell. He thus becomes the Great Enemy, seeking to destroy everything that is good. The Satanic objective is here set down by the poet, whose insight does not fail to explain in what ways the malcontent and revolutionary consoles himself with further acts of defiant malice—as futile as they are senseless. What sort of being does not know its proper place? What sort of being is drawn into an abyss by prideful error, undeterred by the hopelessness of his position? It is fanciful poetry, some would say. But no, it was astute psychology to set it down. Satan's character, thus drawn by Milton, may be seen as the character of the New Religion, which has so cunningly perverted everything it touches. Here is an entry into Hell. Here is a place made by its own inhabitants—made miserable by choice.

> The mind is its own place, and in itself
> Can make a Heaven of Hell, a Hell of Heaven.[32]

Heaven and Hell are not places, strictly speaking. The Abode of Light and the Abode of Darkness represent and reflect the condition of the souls that dwell therein. The punishments and tortures suffered in Hell are of our own devising. Wounded by the thought of his smallness next to God, Satan rebelled and fell from Heaven to a place that spiritually mirrored his own inner condition. Returning God's love with envious hate, Satan is tortured and crushed by the futility of his own wickedness. He has not learned that love drives out power in equal measure as power drives out love. Thus Satan finds himself in Hell, which is a place devoted to power yet devoid of love. "Fall'n Cherube," says Satan to Beelzebub, "to be weak is miserable."[33] To be powerful is therefore everything. According to Satan, Hell is preferable:

> Here we may reign secure; and, in my choice,
> To reign is worth ambition, though in Hell:
> Better to reign in Hell than serve in Heaven.[34]

History is dotted with negating spirits of this type. Their legacy of evil cannot be denied. What is worth noting, however, is the appearance of thousands or millions of such spirits during the last century, flooding into every field of endeavor. It is as if Hell had unleashed a mass of demons, in rising sequence, flooding into the world. Toxic devils in the form of human beings!

It must be admitted that we have enabled the wrong sort of people to rise in society—to become our top leaders. More often than not, we do not have the best men in office. It cannot be emphasized too strongly that the malignant narcissist, with his grandiose and compensatory desire for greatness, seeks a position of unchallenged power without checks or balances. If he is exceptionally capable, or receives the help of exceptionally capable people, he can build himself into a monstrous power. The real man behind the façade—however gifted or heroic—is then consumed by the vanities which attend political deification. Under this situation a leader inevitably fails to know himself and his own limitations. Such failure arises out of something more fundamental than a lack of self-knowledge. Perhaps it is cowardice in the face of self-knowledge. Wanting to be a political god signifies an unwillingness to accept oneself; that is, to accept one's own humanity. It suggests an underlying weakness, a desire for something inappropriate. Wanting to be a god is not merely foolish. It is crazy. And in the end, it is evil.

Chapter Four

The Fool and the Hero

> But when I looked into the mirror I cried out and my heart
> was shaken: for I did not see myself, I saw the sneer and
> grimace of a devil.
>
> — Friedrich Nietzsche[35]

Putrefaction

Corruption leads to demoralization and a sick society. *That which becomes sick falls prey.* Here is the process by which empires fall and
nations die. Corruption enters society on a stream of "new" ideas.
Perversion gains admittance. The taint spreads. Venality and dishonesty are
doubled—then redoubled. Immorality reigns. The honest man is punished
for telling the truth. The legions abandon the frontier.

A nation is defended, overtly, by its armed forces and police. Its spiritual
continuance, however, depends on more subtle formations. These are not
tank battalions or infantry regiments, but teachings and principles, ideals and
moral insights. If *these* are corrupted and transmuted into false teachings and
evil principles, no armed force will prove sufficient in defense; for those forces
would be inwardly undone.

The New Religion, wherever and whenever it appears, is a corrupt teaching. Its progress is guided by an infallible subversive sense. Its idealism may
contain elements of truth, but the effect is to weaken society in advance of
killing it. For example, deny that women should be mothers. Say, instead,
that motherhood is slavery. Say that sex is about pleasure, not procreation.
Say that there is no soul, no higher dimension of spirit, no supernatural. By
saying such things, you cut off the next generation. You foreshorten the family. You eliminate the soul. You strip life of higher meaning and leave man

with the satisfactions of physical pleasure alone. By saying such things you turn man into an empty shell, a hedonist, a spiritual cripple.

If a society wishes to survive, then woman must again be mother. Man must again be father. Marriage must again be the union of male and female. The soul must again be acknowledged. That which is highest and best must be honored. Once upon a time we traveled within ourselves. We received inspiration from the Muses.* We received visions and divine messages. We knew that a higher intelligence was guiding our course. We believed in life after death. And now, with the corruption of our ideas, we believe in nothing; that is, we believe in a Godless theory which postulates creation without a creator.

The New Faith says that humanity evolved out of dead matter. Purposing nothing, the dead hand of a lifeless universe made man on accident—an unintended consequence of chemical reactions. That is the theory of the New Religion. There is not one shred of evidence for this theory. It is monstrous and absurd. Yet it is the accepted gospel, the prevailing idea, the basis for the cultural changes we see around us today. The New Religion claims that life was born out of nonlife—out of a mindless universal chaos, out of the swirling of cosmic atoms, the crashing of planets, the exploding of suns. A cacophony without meaning! This is what the atheist says about our creation. Of course, we must not say that man was created, for that would imply a Creator and this is what the New Religion denies. We are now taught to say that man has "evolved." Yet the thing he evolved out of must prove less and less significant, the theory being that the further back in time the less complex the organism—until you arrive at an ancestor that is not an organism at all. First there is the knuckle-dragging primate; then an animal walking on all fours; then a tiny rat-like creature. Eventually one finds man's ancestor to be a bug or worm—a thing that crawls. Go back another two billion years and you find a squiggly microscopic ancestor. But the evolutionist cannot stop there. He must continue to shrink and simplify until, logically, he pretends to have discovered our ultimate ancestor—a thing immeasurably small and stupid as the father of all. But then, the infinite evolutionary regress cannot stop there. It must continue until we reach nothing at all.

The atheistic faith moves, step by step, toward this universal neutering— this *nihilism*. Life is here conceived without conception. It is the "immaculate conception" of something out of nothing. Aristotle and the ancients knew better. They knew that mankind was a creature made by a Creator. But modern man has discarded metaphysics as nonsense. We have built radio telescopes to search for intelligent life in outer space; but we have failed to realize that our own DNA, which is the most sophisticated coded sequence known to man, *proves* the existence of an extramundane intelligence. Quite

* These are the goddesses who inspire literature, science and the arts.

obviously, DNA is not noise. It is information; and where there is information there must be an originator of information—a mind that existed before the human mind. And more importantly, *a mind that does not depend upon DNA for its existence!*

The New Religion has many arguments with which to impugn metaphysics. A monkey banging on a typewriter for a billion years might, say the evolutionists, compose the works of Shakespeare on accident. Such a monkey might also tap out DNA. Everything becomes possible in a random universe after billions of years of "monkey business."

Two objections will suffice: (1) Who will make and train a monkey to type; and (2) who will build the typewriter? There is no passage from the chaotic swirl of atom and molecule to a living intelligent being (let alone a typewriter). Would geologists, finding a typewriter imbedded in million-year-old sedimentary strata assume it was "naturally" produced by the rock? Why, then, would we think that some giant rock (called Earth) could produce DNA?

Is it rational to postulate a human race that belongs to no one, that comes from nothing, that is journeying nowhere? In essence, this is the view of the New Religion. Here is a device for breaking the internal motor of man, for striking at man's dignity, for denying man's spiritual significance, and for denying *that* which stands above man. Here we return to the idea of subversion; for how else could the criminal, the misfit and the rebel take hold of God's office? How else could he make himself the center of the universe?

Once a man has become the center of the universe, what limits will he observe? What law will he follow? What will constrain his vanity, his lust, his arrogance? The human race is not God. Not even public opinion is God. But now, under the New Religion, we dispense with the Old Religion. We deny that man possesses God-given instincts. We deny that women are women and men are men. We deny our essence as creatures. And so we have lost touch with the source of our being—the Creator. The New Religion, by its campaign of eradicating the sacred, brings us to a critical situation: *The loss of the Holy Grail.* In the mythology of the Grail we are confronted with a dying world. Redemption can only occur if the Grail is recovered by a knight who is pure of heart; that is to say, by someone whose thoughts and feelings are good and untainted.

Few realize that the land is dying—*that our race is dying.* Such a suggestion may seem over-dramatic. But look more carefully at the world around us. Look at the acceleration of dysfunction, disorder and discord. Motherhood is no longer sacred, but cursed. Manhood is not honored, but dishonored. Abortion is made legal. The future does not matter. The past is dismissed as irrelevant. There is only the howling fanatic, the political tract of the feminist, the socialist, the egalitarian, the social worker, the state and its agents—the usurpers of God's office. The state, indeed, is a jealous god. It is jealous of the father; but also, jealous of the mother and desirous of total control over the child. The strategy behind the game is the strategy of separating the child from his parents. But first, disconnect the parents from each other. Disconnect the woman from the man. Disconnect the children from the woman. Then *make man in your own image.*

The New Religion is cunning in its demagoguery. It uses lust as a weapon, ambition as a weapon, jealousy as a weapon. Materialism and atheism are also weapons. The New Religion has broken society's mechanism of regeneration—*the family.* The New Religion doesn't care about mankind. Its high priests want power over creation. They want control over history. It must be intoxicating to guide the destiny of mankind, to usurp God, to rewrite the Ten Commandments. But do the high priests of the New Religion know what they are doing? In departing from the ancient customs and folkways, have they not departed from a higher common sense? Have they not erred? Have they not paved a highway to Hell? One cannot say, with confidence, that the New Religion has put anything to good order. We look at the world they have begun to build and we see, quite plainly, that it doesn't work. The mixing of alien peoples in the name of mankind doesn't work. Gay marriage doesn't work. Socialism doesn't work. Feminism doesn't work. Abortion doesn't work. What madman would say that these things are good? These ideas signify the demoralization and depopulation of society. In a word, they signify "death." To repeat the analysis: Corruption leads to demoralization and a sick society. *That which becomes sick falls prey.* Here is the process by which empires fall and nations die.

If a child has a future, it is only because benevolent beings—called parents—are watching over him. Many parents are inspired to protect their children from evil; to inculcate the good, the beneficial, and the necessary. What kind of parents would do otherwise? And what ideas form the basis of the child's orientation? What ideas do parents, by nature, want to instill? Do not imagine that natural instinct—the profound inspiration of the parent—creates a desire to make a little boy into a little girl. There is, indeed, a natural order, a natural desire—a teleology which reveals itself to the parent. By nature the mother defends her young with great ferocity. The prudence of the father sees far ahead, anticipating future threats. Here is the idea of defense at its most basic level, the basis for the "conscript father" and the patriot of every country. Ask yourself why this idea has come under assault.

Patriarchy isn't something bad, and neither is patriotism. The words patriarchy and patriotism refer to the role of the father. The father of a country is its protector. No fathers, no protectors. A society is defended by men, and relies for its defense on the fighting instinct of the man; for men have always made their wars into games and their games into wars. The Iliad is not an epic poem about metrosexual*s* getting in touch with their feminine side. Always and ever, the truly great culture respects man and woman *as they are*—not by drawing an equal sign between them with which to engender an unholy un-differentiation.

The fool who accepts the equating of male with female must fall prey to a whole train of false principles and doctrines. His politics carries him away from common sense. His corruption is progressive and steady. He must end by hating his father and distrusting his own instincts. He becomes the opposite of a patriot; that is to say, his instincts point in the direction of treason. He breaks down his country at every opportunity. He favors the alien, the misfit, the homosexual. He squanders the legacy of his ancestors. He leaves nothing for his children—if he has children at all. He is a non-defender, a neuter, a hen-pecked, sorry, weak, pathetic, self-justifying suicide.

What is the opposite of potency? One might say impotency. That which seeks to replace nature with its own program must strike down potency; for the potent follow nature. But the enemy of nature says *no*. Do not "be fruitful and multiply." *We* who are against the instinctual things of this world wish to make a new world, entirely determined by ourselves. We envy that which gives life, that which is deep and unfathomable. We are against the flowers that open toward the sun. *We are* the New Sun. It is only permissible that flowers open their petals toward *us*!

Our confusion knows no bounds whatsoever. Our ideas have been corrupted by an ideology which we take to be true. We do not as yet recognize how false our thinking has become. Our corruption runs so deep, and is so all-pervading, that marriage no longer signifies the union of man and woman. We no longer respect fatherhood. Therefore, we no longer value patriotism or patriarchy. It follows that we accept Islam as a "religion of peace." Our lexicon now reserves the word "enemy" for the Islamophobe, the homophobe, and the anticommunist. Defense is now impossible. The manly functions of the state fall into decline or disuse. The nanny state—a feminine construction—rises up. Instead of statesmen and warriors we have committees of women managing a welfare bureaucracy. The masses are hereby infantilized, turned back into children. Mommy now bakes cookies on a government salary. The state is her husband. The indigent are her children. The entire system is a perversion of the natural order.

Under this system the fool no longer recognizes his enemy. Year by year the fool forgets his military readiness. He eats the cookies prepared for him by the nanny state. Weaker and weaker he grows, less and less in touch with reality. The fool always bungles. He does not know how to appreciate anything, or how to estimate the value of anything. The fool, above all, is a moral fool—and immorality his cardinal weakness. He always needs to be encouraged, propped up, or praised. He feeds on the attention of others. The English dictionary defines a fool as "one who shows himself, by words or actions, to be deficient in judgment, sense, or understanding; a stupid or thoughtless person…." Another definition reads, "one who has been or can be easily deceived or imposed upon; a dupe…."

The New Religion was made for our modern fools, and our modern fools were shaped by *it*. Their nature leads them to despise the old wisdom, ancient learning, and the lessons of history. The New Religion offers an easy shortcut to understanding everything through "science." It plays upon their delusions, their childishness, their desire for happy endings and rainbows. The fool cannot be honest with himself. Therefore, he rushes to embrace the well-designed half-truth. Here, self-indulgence makes the fool a co-collaborator in his own deception. He imagines himself moving toward a brave new world. Actually, there is no such world. There is only destruction and death. The core ideas by which human civilizations rise are transcendental, permanent, everlasting truths which cannot be contradicted in safety. Tragically, the fool listens to and is tickled by those who contradict common sense. The New Religion, with the fool as its pupil, must teach that the universe is chaotic, that there is nothing inherently moral in it, that there is no higher intelligence behind it, or guiding it. What has happened heretofore is not creation but evolution—the accidental birth of a god called "man." Only now can creation begin—since humanity has supposedly (by the grace of science) reached full consciousness. The preface to Karl Marx's doctoral thesis contains the following sentences: "The proclamation of Prometheus—'in a word, I hate all the gods'—is [philosophy's] own profession, her own slogan against all the gods of heaven and earth who do not recognize man's self-consciousness as the highest divinity. There shall be no other beside it."[36]

The fool is ready to accept this. He is ready to embark on the greatest catastrophe in all recorded history. He fails to defend what must be defended. He fails to defend the woman, the child, the family, the nation. He embraces cultural Marxism. He embraces nihilism, tempted by the lunacy that he can become a god. This is laughable, of course. Nothing good, in fact, will come of his deification. He will turn civilization into a pile of rubble. He will erase himself, because that is what fools do.

Beyond the Rot

Under normal conditions, the healthy society defends itself. It prepares for war against its enemies. But a corrupt society deludes itself that its enemies are "partners." It negotiates unenforceable treaties, signs ill-advised trade agreements and gives generous humanitarian aid. The politician says that he will "trust but verify." In practice, however, the politician dares not verify. Being made a fool of from the moment he gave his trust, the politician is discredited to such an extent that he dares not speak about the enemy's faithlessness. In politics it is the height of folly to find oneself swindled. What president or prime minister admits to being a jackass? He must hide the fact that he has been tricked; and so, he ends his career by colluding with his enemies.

A sick society refuses to acknowledge the truth. Again and again in history, when a country becomes slack and pleasure-seeking, truth is overtaken by the desire for comfort. People do not want trouble, and proper national defense is full of trouble. So it happens, little by little, that people lie to themselves because it feels good. Once this kind of dishonesty takes root, it grows and spreads. There is no controlling it. One does not dare to warn such a society about its enemies. People who seek pleasure despise Jeremiahs and their jeremiads.* Such people do not respect vigilance, or reward patriotism. More and more, the truth is their enemy.

The fool imagines that politics is about making "heaven on earth." He comes to believe in political solutions to intractable problems. He believes in the establishment of permanent peace, where all men are brothers and all nations are combined into a single nation. Why should there be conflict? Why should men kill each other? Using superficial reasoning, the fool asks such questions and gives out fatuous answers.

Major Gen. J.F.C. Fuller, one of the leading military theorists of the twentieth century, once wrote: "Rightly or wrongly, I do not believe that war can be eliminated, because it is part and parcel of life; for life in its broadest meaning is the shifting outcome of destructive and constructive propensities."[37] More could be said along these lines. Man is not a peaceful animal, but a quarrelsome animal. The "war to end all wars" was a farce, loaded with hypocrisy.[38] There can be no end of war. In every situation, man finds himself in the same troubled circumstance. The various tribes of the Earth are not brothers, and they never will be brothers. And even if they were all brothers, did not Cain kill Abel? Did not Romulus kill Remus? How many times in history has brother killed brother?

---

* Jeremiah the prophet began his work in Judah midway through the reign of Josiah (640-609 B.C.). Jeremiah was famous for decrying the sins of his countrymen.

47

It is often said that "war is evil." Why not dispense with this evil by pushing it out of our minds? Some now preach that we ought to forget about war as if forgetfulness promised a cure. But those who believe in "the power of positive thinking" have made a mistake if they deny the reality of conflict. Reality is something that doesn't go away when you stop thinking about it. Before one can deal with a problem, one must acknowledge that the problem exists. The primary problem, of course, is not war. The primary problem is enmity; the fact that men have enemies, and enemies often fight each other. This reality is as inescapable as death and taxes. There is no way out of it.

The state is responsible for defending society from its enemies. But we have diverted the state into a very different set of activities (that is, playing mommy). The state's legitimacy is now supposedly built upon the idea of making everyone equal—providing everyone with an education, healthcare and subsistence in old age. For some time military spending has had to give way to "social spending." As society becomes addicted to social spending, military spending is choked off. It is no accident that those demanding more and more social spending are traditionally associated with the enemies of the West. It is only natural that these enemies should want to weaken the West militarily. Therefore, as democracy becomes more and more hedonistic we see that military spending declines. Thus Europe is unwilling to keep up with Russia's military buildup. The United States also continues to weaken. The trend toward democratic hedonism signals disarmament. No longer will the hedonist defend his nation. In fact, he will proudly invite millions of hostile aliens to share his country. He will not defend his borders, his language or his culture.

One must carefully examine the political rhetoric of the so-called "peace party." During the Vietnam War protestors burned the American flag and hoisted the Vietcong flag. One might call such people "peace protesters," but in reality they were not in favor of peace. They favored the enemy. Similarly, those in Europe today who favor "tolerance" toward Muslims are actually taking the side of Islam. Such "tolerance" is not really about peace or the brotherhood of man. In practice, it is about improving the position of one religion over another; for those who favor tolerance do not enter Saudi Arabia and demand an opening for Christians and Hindus in the land of the Prophet. If they seriously did so, then we might credit them as preachers of tolerance. But as long as tolerance is a one way street, it is nothing but hypocrisy and self-deception.

Peace is a funny thing. Everyone says they want peace and, of course, they do. Only they want peace on their own terms. Ironically this is the purpose of war—to dictate the terms of peace. Men cannot always agree and therefore resolve their differences by fighting. This is unavoidable. Many ideologists today believe that their pet ideas will bring peace to mankind. The capitalists believe that universal democracy and the free market will bring peace. The socialists believe that the destruction of capitalism will bring peace. But there will not be peace. There will always be wars. Vain are those theories that talk of "world government" or global disarmament. It is childish to believe in a Peace Fairy. But people want to believe. They want to believe that history—as a series of wars—will someday end. Francis Fukuyama actually wrote a book titled *The End of History*.[39] Fukuyama suggested that capitalism and the ballot box would solve the problem of the haves and have-nots. Of course, the true-believer in liberal democracy is bound to think along these lines.

The problem with Fukuyama, of course, is that there is no "end of history" as he imagined it. Democratic capitalism was never a panacea. Contrary to the prevailing nonsense, democracy is merely another way of organizing oligarchy. To make a religion out of democracy, or out of the free market, is very stupid. Nevertheless, Fukuyama's book was hailed with great fanfare as a "modern classic." But there was nothing classical about it. Quite decisively the book debunks itself by "referring to the creature who reportedly emerges [triumphant] at the end of history, the *last man*."[40] And who is the last man? He is *the fool of history*. The *last man* was described long ago by Friedrich Nietzsche as the end product of egalitarian levelling. As such, the *last man* is "the most contemptible man ... the man who can no longer despise himself!" The *last man* does not aspire, but is self-satisfied and weak. "The Earth has become small, and upon it hops the Last Man, who makes everything small. His race is ineradicable as the flea; the Last Man lives longest."[41] He is smug, small, ignoble, numerous—a creature less than human: domesticated, lacking instinct, inferior, irreligious, bored. According to Fukuyama, Nietzsche's *last man* was "in essence, a victorious slave."[42] Fukuyama does not refute Nietzsche's critique of democratic egalitarianism. He merely dismisses Nietzsche as "an opponent of democracy." What is wrong, asks Fukuyama, with becoming comfortable, self-satisfied and prosperous? Fukuyama finally says, "It is difficult for those of us who believe in liberal democracy to follow Nietzsche very far down the road that he takes."[43] Here, Fukuyama, as *last man*, dares not think *beyond* himself. Fukuyama's rhetorical defense of the bourgeoisie is sensible enough; yet he is suggesting that these same people, who "sold the rope" by which their enemies will hang them, have a bright future. He does not, therefore, deal with the problem of liberalism's failure. He simply evades the problem, as if evasion were a method for escaping danger. But evasion is not a valid way out. It is merely something *last men* indulge in.

Like nearly all pundits today, Fukuyama could not see to the heart of the problem. He praised democracy and capitalism as opening the door to a period of unprecedented peace. Why else would he append this formula to "the end of history"? The truth that people do not want to hear, which is painful and unpleasant, is that *there is no political salvation for man.* The problem with so many pundits, and so many enthusiasts, is their inability to digest reality. Man is a fool, and fools are not saved by their political doings. Rather, their political doings *constantly endanger them.* In politics the fool is merely translated from one state of distress to another. This occurs continuously, and is the stuff of history.

Nietzsche saw what the ideological liberal can never see; namely, that liberalism contains within itself the seeds of its own destruction. The twenty-first century reader need only look around. Are not the barbarians preparing to sack Rome? Look at what is happening in Germany, in America, in Brazil—in all civilized countries. Did Francis Fukuyama see any of this coming? He does not even see it now, when it has become visible to all but those who are besotted with the old ideology. There is no "end of history." There is only the end of mankind.

War is always going to be with us. The ever-present possibility of war gives us the very grounds of our political order. Political order is born in war, and dies in war. This implies that all peoples at all times have enemies. One must be careful, of course, to avoid paranoia—yet there is truth in the dictum that nations are born in blood. Carl Schmitt noted, "It would be ludicrous to believe that a defenseless people has nothing but friends, and it would be a deranged calculation to suppose that the enemy could perhaps be touched by the absence of a resistance."[44]

It is terribly unfortunate to be undefended. What better invitation could there be for an attacker?

Men will always find causes for enmity. They will always make war on each other. It is a delusion to think otherwise. Men will be enemies. Denial cannot prevent this. Always and ever, man must confront his enemy. He must stand or fall. He must defend his kith and kin. This was true three thousand years ago. It is true today. Those who flatter themselves that we have outgrown wars are the worst of our modern fools; for they do not know themselves or the stuff of which they are made. Look around and see. The present craze for appeasing Muslims stems from a general ignorance of history and human nature. The same can be said about Europe's disarmament in the face of Russia's rapid rearmament. The fool denies that he has an enemy. He puts his own existence at risk. Corrupt ideas have annihilated his sense of self-preservation.

The fool of today is someone who has lost his instincts. He cannot tell friend from foe. He dwells in an eternal present, with banner headlines that pass very quickly, and soundbites, and news clips. The fool cannot relate his knowledge to any larger historical context. Everyone is thought to be similar. To identify differences is bigotry. To recognize that man is tribal, and the tribes of the earth are always at war, is dismissed as propaganda from the "military industrial complex." But it isn't propaganda. It is the truth.

The fool's ideology stands wisdom on its head. Whatever has been true from time immemorial is said to be untrue. The fool believes that human problems can be solved with science, that war is unnecessary, that poverty can be eliminated, that social evils can be cured with better schools and higher pay for teachers. The fool commits himself to many utopian projects. Wealth is confiscated through taxation and squandered on these same idiotic projects. "We are improving human nature," the fool says to himself. In the final analysis we find that human nature cannot be refashioned by fools. Rather, the fool is fated to play out the comedy occasioned by his foolishness. Alas, he does not know that he is a fool. He cannot stop himself from making foolish mistakes. He cannot read history without thinking to himself that he can do better (only to do worse). The modern fool believes himself to be exempt from the laws of history. After all, he is enlightened. But then, he always thought himself enlightened. Never has he admitted the truth about himself. Never did he cringe at his ignorance, or recoil in horror at his follies. Neither did he look in a mirror to see the devil staring back. Always he prettified his condition, lied about his qualifications, and justified his actions. And so his blindness has always been absolute, all-determining, all-encompassing. The fool thinks that foolishness is what *other* people do.

What is required in all ages is prudence. This is not a virtue which fools possess. Furthermore, prudence does not consist in what Thomas Carlyle called "Beaver Intelligence." It consists, instead, in a generalizing capacity, an integrative ability which makes wholes out of parts. The political function, the strategic function, depends on our ability to generalize and integrate. It requires the rank ordering of things and people. This is the function which, together with intellectual integrity, is absolutely essential today. And it is lacking.

There are men who are a treasure, who are filled with energy and courage and keen perceptiveness and reverence. All these things, being properly ordered within, are reflected in outward doings. The vulgar multitude does not always recognize such men at the outset. However, greatness is always recognized in the end. This is the narrow passage from sickness back to health. Today's preoccupation with celebrities cannot last forever. *Changes will come.* Society will learn from its mistakes—or it will perish.

The fool is always with us, of course. But he will not always be on top. Civilization owes its existence to the wise and brave—to the men of virtue. A heroic leader lends his good instincts, his sense of order, to the whole people. His powers are palliative, healing and uplifting. He paves the way toward a better future. Thomas Carlyle wrote of him,

We cannot look, however imperfectly, upon a great man without gaining something by him. He is the living light-fountain, which it is good and pleasant to be near. The light which enlightens, which has enlightened the darkness of the world; and this not as a kindled lamp only, but rather as a natural luminary shining by the gift of Heaven; a flowing light-fountain, as I say, of native original insight, of manhood and heroic nobleness—in whose radiance all souls feel that it is well with them.

This is our remedy, in human form. It is the grace of God. It is the fool being put in his place—set aside in favor of someone better.

Chapter Five

THE WINEPRESS OF THE WRATH OF GOD

He who is truly and hopelessly little will always drag the revelation of the greater down to the level of his littleness, and will never understand that the day of judgment for his littleness has dawned.

— Carl Jung[45]

A spirit of negation, wearing many masks and telling many lies, has come into its own as an organized power. It fosters corruption and feeds on human weakness. It is metaphysically aligned with evil even as it denies the metaphysics of evil. It is a kind of organized crime that has entered into politics, philosophy and the arts. It is armed with all the intellectual weapons of the age. Its malevolent genius stands above the human herd, targeting the resistance of the individual—hoping to eradicate the individual. Only an organized counterforce, which has yet to appear, could ever threaten it.

The goal of this evil spirit is to pervert human nature. To accomplish this it is sufficient to belittle all great and wonderful ideas, to pour the acid of contempt upon goodness and cynically dismiss honesty as a kind of dishonesty. The method here is to direct the heart of man against itself; to foul the everyday thoughts of ordinary people; to redirect the best and brightest toward negation as if this were a path to liberation. This entire program, disguised as something good and "progressive," claims to be historically necessary. But there is nothing necessary here. What, after all, is necessary about breaking the link between one generation and another? What is necessary about a son turning against his father? Naturally, the future must find itself entirely disconnected and cut off. The spirit of negation seeks such a break, such a disintegration of soul, through revolutionary discontinuity—reducing man to a pitiable creature who cannot judge what is right or true because he has lost his wider context.

The spirit of negation advances a creed of negation (i.e., revolution). This creed is a snare. The man who adopts it is destined to turn against himself. Such is the significance of our manifold perversions. All perversion, all psychological disorder, adds up to suicide. Being against themselves, the spiritually perverted instinctively erect a regime of self-hatred and self-blame. They open the gates of the Sacred City to their enemy. The unconscious tendency of their unacknowledged self-loathing shows itself in a thousand ways, refracted through the prism of a self-immolating policy. The regime *of* the little man, *by* the little man, and *for* the little man passes judgment on itself. It has no greatness, no truth, no instinct, no true spirituality. Everything here is out of kilter. Everything is amiss.

The little man, believing in his equality with great men, does not see that his course has become dangerous. He does not admit, "I cannot navigate this path." With no higher power to turn to, and no hero to save him, he blunders his way forward. He says there is no revelation. He announces God's death. He moves into God's office. He looks at the inequalities which exist between idiot and Genius. *He takes the side of the idiot.* He says that no one should be "better" than anyone else. As a charlatan who seeks ultimate power for himself, he presents his counterfeit of order—*egalitarianism*—as the basis of a new order; that is to say, he opens the door to *socialism*.

Under socialism the little man eschews the man of judgment and prudence, the godsend of Providential Grace. Instead of a godsend we find an envious despoiler of the rich—an ambitious rabble rouser obsessed with getting power. Such are always ready to push their way in, loudly proclaiming the "rights" of the little man; loudly demanding equality for the poor and downtrodden. This is the demagogy of a rising totalitarianism, fueled by envy and ambition. The political criminal who founds such a regime does not accept the ordering of a Greater Being. He insists on ascending God's throne. At first he proclaims the rights of the workers and peasants. In the end he advances the cause of the immigrant and the alien, the homosexual and the Muslim. He wants to redistribute everyone's wealth. His bureaucracy reaches to Heaven. Everything is given to him for the purpose of rearrangement. This is how he remakes the world.

In ancient times Caesar was proclaimed a god, and was satisfied with commanding armies and leading a government. Today's Caesar wants to have power over humanity in a way that Julius Caesar never dreamed. It is not enough for the small man to be proclaimed a god, or to command the government. He must exercise an arbitrary power over every aspect of human life and economy. He must even pretend to control the weather.* There must

---

* Changing the climate by reducing everyone's "carbon footprint."

be no practical limit to his exercise of power. And there is no telling what he will demand next. The day will inevitably dawn when he decides there are too many people inhabiting the earth. Then he will say how many billions live and how many billions die.

The new Caesars have already negated hundreds of millions of lives. "One death is a tragedy," said Stalin. "One million deaths is a statistic." The small man becomes great by way of mass murder. The negation of the many proves the superiority of the little men with their big bureaucracy. If the world will not affirm them, then they will take revenge upon the world. Therefore is murder their self-affirmation. If only such men could accept their smallness. If only they could happily embrace the many advantages and compensations that Nature offers to the small. But this is not acceptable to those possessed of outsized egos. They cannot think in proper proportion. The word "destruction" rattles through them like a prayer to Hell.

Even as these words are written, the negating spirit grows and spreads as it prepares to consume the nations. The greatest calamity in all history is now on its way. The spirit of negation, with its vanguard of small men, precipitates a global unravelling. Out of this, with the Grace of God, the revolutionary vanguard itself will be annihilated by the very forces that they have unleashed.

Here we find a process. It is the cyclical process of death and rebirth. The springtime brings life to Nature. The summer is glorious. Autumn sees the promised harvest, followed by the darkness of winter. But winter is not the end of life. It is merely the end of one cycle, one year. So it is with the ages of man. The darkness which lengthens before the winter solstice does not signify doomsday. It signifies a period of hibernation that precedes the return of spring. It is the three days of darkness that prefigure resurrection.

There are also cycles within nations and civilizations. A process of death and rebirth also plays out in history. In the case of Western civilization the end of our cycle was long ago prefigured by those small-souled hominids with gargantuan brains—like Karl Marx and Charles Darwin—who inspired men who were smaller still, evermore tediously crawling on all fours, reverting, degenerating—like Sigmund Freud, Jacques Derrida and Jürgen Habermas, toward the smug nihilism of a mass grave. We often hear of religious frauds and imposters, but who has dared laugh openly at those secular frauds—those intellectual "giants" of our time—living on the cutting edge of charlatanism? These bear witness to modernity's shameful credulity. Putting it another way: There may be charm in the meanest religious superstition; but our secular superstition is attended by unreadable prose, dull argument, and bloated abstraction. There is no warmth, no springtime in these secularists. Quite obviously, they are harbingers of winter—of increasing darkness and frozen landscape.

Our degenerate society celebrates these masters of intellectual convolution, academic nihilism and secular mystification. It is only natural that our time identifies with such souls—accepting them as good and wise. Later ages will forget them entirely. When the darkness has passed, and the light returns, nobody will read these boring people. Their spirit of negation being overcome, another spirit will prevail. New conflicts and struggles will begin, of course. But these will not be dripping with as much mischief and envy. Men will have to wait another fifteen hundred years for *that*.

Therefore, why should we despair? Is there no rainbow after the storm? You might say this is poor consolation for those drowned in the Flood. But we live in a world of good and bad things, of creation and destruction, of rain and rainbows, of dark ages and golden ages. Must we see the glass as "half empty"? And must our egotism grant us a golden age—though we have earned no such thing? The revelation is, as always, that the bankrupt must face bankruptcy. And here we are referring to *spiritual* bankruptcy. As of this moment, as these words are written, a Great Calamity lies ahead of us. Evidence of the disintegration of our civilization is on every side. The regime of self-loathing, led by small men, already rules by a policy of negation. There is no way out of the impasse excepting that path described in visionary teachings.

It says in the Bible, "Where *there is* no vision, the people perish…."[46] This is what it comes down to—tools of spiritual insight provided by Heaven, by angelic visitation, by signs in the skies. Characteristically, the small man misidentifies these signs. The angelic messenger is now mistaken for an extraterrestrial. The Spirit of God must be susceptible to radar. After all, man's soul has been explained by our toilet training; and Freud's sexual theory now serves as a bulwark "against the black tide … of occultism."[47]

In terms of the historical drama which unfolds before us, the black tide of occultism has something to say. It was, indeed, Niccolò Machiavelli—reputedly the first political scientist*—who wrote a section under the heading, "Before Great Misfortunes befall a City or a Province they are preceded by Portents or foretold by Men." Here Machiavelli shows that the black tide of the occult has always been with us, and *shall* always be with us. And if Machiavelli is the inspiration of the modern political scientists, well, they ought to pay closer attention to what he *actually* said:

> How it comes about I know not, but it is clear from ancient and modern cases that no serious misfortune ever befalls a city or a province that has not been predicted either by divination

---

* In contrast with Aristotle's norm-laden politics, Machiavelli sought political truth in direct opposition to morality. This supposedly distinguishes him as "scientific"—as if science is bound to eschew the normative, per Max Weber's "Wissenschaft als Beruf."

or revelation or by prodigies or by other heavenly signs. There is no need to go far afield to prove this. Everybody knows how, before King Charles VIII of France came to Italy, his coming was frequently foretold by Friar Girolamo Savonarola, and how, in addition to this, it was said that armed hosts had been heard and seen in the sky above Arezzo fighting one with the other.[48]

Machiavelli said that the cause of such events "should be discussed and explained" by those who are versed "in things natural and supernatural...." Admittedly he was not so versed. Nonetheless Machiavelli suggested, "It may be, of course, as some philosophers would have it, that the atmosphere is full of spirits, endowed by nature with the virtue to foresee the future, who out of sympathy for men give them warning by means of such signs so that they may look to their defense."[49]

A psychiatrist, who *was* versed in things "natural and supernatural," named Carl Jung, wrote a book titled *Flying Saucers, A Modern Myth of Things Seen in the Sky*. He warned that a "political, social, philosophical, and religious conflict of unprecedented proportions has split the consciousness of our age." He noted that "the need for a savior will make itself felt."[50] Having examined a number of UFO dreams, he came upon one that involved "a disk-like Ufo manned by spirits, a space-ship that comes out of the beyond to the edge of our world in order to fetch the souls of the dead." Jung then said "that the Ufo might be a sort of Charon."[51] This suggestion was "hardly surprising," perhaps obvious. Yet nobody had offered it as an explanation—not merely because they lacked knowledge of Greek mythology, but modern men are not likely to accept such "disagreeable conclusions." According to Jung,

> The apparent increase in UFO sightings in recent years has caused disquiet in the popular mind and might easily give rise to the conclusion that, if so many space–ships appear from the beyond, a corresponding number of deaths may be expected. We know that such phenomenon were interpreted like this in earlier centuries: they were portents of a 'great dying,' of war and pestilence, like the dark premonitions that underlie our modern fear.[52]

Even though we won't admit the truth on one level, it comes to us on another level. As if to confirm Jung's thesis, UFO abductees have noted the presence of dead people onboard flying saucers. The UFO abductee, Whitley Strieber, was shown a vision of the world blowing up. He said he did not know why an alien would show him "images of the future of our world" adding that

these were "the most dreadful images."[53] The intrepid and ever-reflective abductee, the late Karla Turner, wrote of warnings and prophecies concerning
"a coming time of battle,"[54] and "the human diaspora."[55] The future was going
to be violent. Certain individuals would have tasks to perform before being
killed. One UFO message read, "Children of the northern peoples, you wander in impenetrable darkness. Your mother mourns."[56]

The French-born UFO researcher, Jacques Vallee, has noted that "a certain number of consistent rumors play a role in the unfolding of the total
myth."[57] He added, "flying saucers, real or not as objects, clearly introduce a
central element in an already troubled future landscape."[58] This is undeniably
true; and there is a curious relationship between this "troubled landscape" and
things that go bump in the night. We know that Jung himself was plagued
with dreams and visions of a future catastrophe. Shortly before his death in
1961, Jung experienced a series of visions of a global cataclysm. According
to Marie-Louise von Franz, the custodian of notes concerning these visions,
Jung foresaw "a worldwide catastrophe, possibly in the nature of a fiery holo-
caust, occurring in about fifty years…."[59]

In the realm of spirit, where the deepest insights are found, the future
may be more clearly seen. What the Jungians call the "unconscious," or the
"collective unconscious," is a realm apart. The unconscious reveals its inner
workings through dreams and visions, supernatural occurrences and synchronicities. Here we must affirm Machiavelli's aforementioned point that "no
serious misfortune" befalls a city or nation "that has not been predicted … by
divination or revelation…." America's Civil War president, Abraham Lincoln,
spoke of such experiences. After learning that he'd been elected president in
1860, he twice saw a deathly image of himself in a mirror. Lincoln interpreted
this to mean that he would not leave office alive. He also had a precognitive
dream ten days before his assassination at the hands of John Wilkes Booth.
Lincoln related his dream to a small gathering of friends on 13 April 1865:

> About ten days ago I retired very late. I had been up waiting
> for important dispatches from the front. I could not have been
> long in bed when I fell into a slumber, for I was weary. I soon
> began to dream. There seemed to be a death-like stillness about
> me. Then I heard subdued sobs, as if a number of people were
> weeping. I thought I left my bed and wandered downstairs.
> Then the silence was broken by the same pitiful sobbing, but
> the mourners were invisible. I went from room to room; no
> living person was in sight, but the same mournful sounds
> of distress met me as I passed along. It was light in all the
> rooms; every object was familiar to me; but where were all the
> people who were grieving as if their hearts would break? I was

puzzled and alarmed. What could be the meaning of all this? Determined to find the cause of a state of things so mysterious and so shocking, I kept on until I arrived at the East Room, which I entered. There I met with a sickening surprise. Before me was a catafalque, on which rested a corpse wrapped in funeral vestments. Around it were stationed soldiers who were acting as guards; and there was a throng of people, some gazing mournfully upon the corpse, whose face was covered, others weeping pitifully. 'Who is dead in the White House?' I demanded of one of the soldiers. 'The President,' was his answer; 'he was killed by an assassin!' Then came a loud burst of grief from the crowd.'[60]

When Lincoln finished telling this dream his wife, Mary, burst out, "That is horrid! I wish you had not told it." Lincoln attempted to calm his wife: "Well, it is only a dream, Mary. Let us say no more about it, and try to forget it." Lincoln was shot the next day, April 14. He died on April 15. On Wednesday, 19 April, Lincoln was placed in a flower-covered catafalque in the East Room of the White House.

The devotees of atheism and the New Religion may mock, but the world is not the stuff of matter alone. It is spirit and mind. There exists a mystifying realm of strange objects, symbols, and prophecies. Today we deny the spirit. We push it out of the way, crediting conscious reason with all the answers. But conscious reason is half an answer. Our ideological and theological preconceptions, our intellectual errors, are many. We *think* we know. Time and again our reason leads us to believe in illusions made of argument and the half-knowledge we think is full knowledge. Through all this the unconscious mind, observing silently from the shadows, sees the danger that has been rationalized into non-danger. It sees the approaching end of the argument. The unconscious mind is not perfect. It is not omniscient. But it sees and reports what it sees—crying out in our sleep, in the midst of our dreams.

The devotees of the New Religion will say that Lincoln's dream is an apocryphal story, a byproduct of superstition. They scoff at such "stories." They dismiss meaningful coincidences. Yet the telltale of the supernatural is far from exhausted by Lincoln's precognitive dream. How strange is a universe that produces synchronicities like those found connecting the deaths of presidents Lincoln and Kennedy?* Consider the following points: Both presidents were elected in 60 (1860 and 1960 respectively). Both had been elected to Congress in 46. Both were shot in the head from behind, on a Friday (by a southerner) before a major holiday while seated next to their wives.

---

* The facts are may be checked by anyone who cares to investigate.

Both presidents were succeeded by southerners named "Johnson" born in 08. Lincoln was shot in a theatre and his assassin was tracked to a warehouse (tobacco barn). Kennedy was shot from a warehouse (book depository) and his assassin was apprehended in a theatre. Both assassins were killed before a trial could be held. Booth was killed with a single shot from a Colt revolver. Oswald was killed with a single shot from a Colt revolver.* The doctors who *first* treated the wounds of Lincoln and Kennedy were both named Charles.† Lincoln died at the Petersen House (PH). Kennedy died at Parkland Hospital (PH). Booth worked at the theatre where Lincoln was shot. Oswald worked at the warehouse where he shot Kennedy. Even more ridiculous, Lincoln was assassinated while sitting in Ford's theatre. Kennedy was assassinated while sitting in a Lincoln Limousine, made by Ford.

According to Carl Jung, there is a non-causal connecting principal which he called "synchronicity." This refers to events that cannot be causally connected in any way, but are nonetheless connected in a meaningful way. The meaning is often "numinous," and described in the following example:

> When for instance I am faced with the fact that my tram ticket bears the same number as the theatre ticket which I buy immediately afterwards, and I receive that same evening a telephone call during which the same number is mentioned again as a telephone number, then a causal connection between these events seems to me improbable in the extreme, although it is obvious that each must have its own causality. I know, on the other hand, that chance happenings have a tendency to fall into aperiodic groupings—necessarily so, because otherwise there would be only a periodic or regular arrangement of events which would by definition exclude chance.[61]

It is, of course, on the basis of sheer "chance" that such coincidences are chiefly explained. Chance groupings, however, *should* be meaningless. But they are not. In fact, ancient systems of divination are based on the assumption that chance groupings *are* meaningful. In Arthur Schopenhauer's essay, "Transcendent Speculation on the Apparent Deliberateness in the Fate of the Individual,"[62] we are introduced to the idea that causal *and* subjective

---

* Jack Ruby killed Oswald with a .38 Colt Cobra. Boston Corbett shot Booth with a U.S. Army issue 44 Colt revolver.

† Charles Leale treated Lincoln at Ford's theatre. Dr. Charles "Jim" Carrico was the Emergency Room doctor at Parkland Memorial Hospital who first treated Kennedy on 22 November 1963 by inserting an endo-tracheal tube into the president's trachea, securing an airway. Another doctor that treated Kennedy that day was Dr. Charles Baxter. Dr. Charles Crenshaw was also present, and later wrote a conspiracy-oriented book that sensationalized what occurred.

connections exist between the fate of persons; that "both types of connections exist simultaneously and … [may] aligned perfectly … each time the fate of one matches the fate of another, and each is made the hero of his own drama while simultaneously figuring in an alien drama." Strange as it is, the philosopher's statement is suggestive of what we see in the fate of Kennedy as it corresponds to that of Lincoln.

Our lives are like dreams, says Schopenhauer. No doubt there is causality; but there is something else at work, which is far more mysterious. Schopenhauer wrote, "It is confirmed empirically and *a posteriori* by the fact, no longer in doubt, that magnetic somnambulists, persons gifted with second sight, and sometimes even the dreams of ordinary sleep directly and accurately predict future events." Schopenhauer went on to say,

> …all that happens is *not blind* and thus the belief in a connection of events in the course of our lives, as systematic as it is necessary, is a fatalism of a higher order which cannot, like simple fatalism, be demonstrated, but happens possibly to everyone sooner or later ….. We can call this *transcendent fatalism*, as distinct from that which is ordinary and demonstrable.[63]

Schopenhauer maintains that "plan and totality" are not to be found in world history, "but in the life of the individual." A nation is an abstract social contrivance. Despite what collectivists might say to the contrary, the individual is *not* a contrivance. "Therefore," says Schopenhauer, "world history is without direct metaphysical significance; it is really only an accidental configuration."[64] When a man reflects on the details of his life, he sometimes realizes that "everything therein had been mapped out…." The systematic arrangement of the individual's life, therefore, "can be explained partly from the immutability and rigid consistency of the inborn character which invariably brings a man back on to the same track." Since the individual, from his very soul, has metaphysical significance, the world appears everywhere intelligible despite the reign of chance. The mysterious intelligence that undergirds the world has given us a patterned and meaningful set of objects for consideration. In his usual pessimistic vein, Schopenhauer then quotes what Goethe says in *Götz von Berlichingen* (Act V): "We human beings do not direct ourselves; power over us is given to evil spirits which practice their mischievous tricks to our undoing."

Drawn to a similarly dark pessimism, the ufologist John A. Keel wrote several books to validate this same thesis. According to Keel, we are "the cattle of the gods"—a psychic food source for interdimensional monsters. In this spirit Keel wrote, "Demonology is not just another crackpot-ology.

It is the ancient and scholarly study of the monsters and demons who have seemingly coexisted with man throughout history."[65] In Keel's books, countless facts are set down to prove the existence of malevolent interdimensional entities. Keel is not interested in God, or why good things exist. He does not dwell upon the benign aspects of cosmic order. For Keel God is a demonic impersonation. Keel's extreme pessimism leads him to suggest that demonic manifestations pervade all history and provide the supernatural impetus for every religion. In *The Eighth Tower* Keel called these demonic agencies "ultraterrestrials" instead of "extraterrestrials"; inhabitants of the "superspectrum" instead of visitors from "outer space"—entities he characterized as "emotionally unstrung, childlike, even stupid."[66] In another work Keel theorized:

> In earlier times the ultraterrestrials established religions among men that, while they seemed benevolent, introduced the practice of making human sacrifices to the gods. This barbaric sacrificial rite was common throughout Europe, Asia, the Pacific, and South America for thousands of years. Only the finest specimens of the tribe were accepted for sacrifice— beautiful young virgins and muscular young men. In most cultures the victims volunteered. It was in fact a very high honor. They were feted before they were led to a high holy place or the top of a pyramid.[67]

Keel's supernatural cup is half-empty. Of course, his warnings about demon possession and dangerous occult forces should be heeded. Yet we may wonder if he has misjudged those Cherubim with flaming sword standing watch east of Eden, guarding the Tree of Life. Man is not permitted to go wherever he pleases. He cannot eat the fruit of every tree. Here we may find the pessimism of Schopenhauer is more realistic, and compensatory, with an almost Christian insistence on the importance of the individual and indestructibility of the soul. For this indestructibility is the real point, the connecting thread, that runs through that which is most vibrant, most numinous and sacred. Here we find the Christian notion that God cares about each person. It is not that we exist for God to eat us, as Keel imagines. Metaphysics does not tend in that direction. Rather, the central ritual of Christendom has been the drinking of Christ's blood and the eating of *His* body which signifies the opposite situation—*a situation in which man eats of God.*

If man is made in the image of God, and he possesses a soul through which God's creativity and freedom is manifest, then it stands to reason that man must take sustenance from God Himself. And, of further importance, it is from this internal "image of God" that men acquire a true sense of what Schopenhauer called "the frailty, vanity, and dream-like quality of all [material] things...." In this way, noted Schopenhauer, "we become conscious of the eternity" of our own inner being "because it is only in contrast to this that the aforesaid quality of [material] things becomes evident...."[68]

The plain truth, indeed, is that we are a part of something greater—something non-material. We are souls. Our existence is drawn from a vast hierarchy of spirit. We look up to Heaven because, in this hierarchy, we are *not* God. Yet we may partake of the divine substance and thereby live. In the Bible Christ says, "It is written, Man shall not live by bread alone, but by every word that proceedeth out of the mouth of God."[69] And in this context, reflecting upon the grotesque and unnatural disorders of modern society, we cannot help seeing the extent to which modern ideologies have disconnected us from God. In this we may also see an apocalypse, a revelation of destruction, of war and pestilence owing to this same separation.

Man is not a biological automaton. He did not come into existence accidentally, and it is suicide to found a system of government on atheistic assumptions. Yet this is exactly what modern ideology has brought us to. Since man consists of spirit and matter, it is an error to say there is only matter, and to make a religion out of material causality; for that is what the Marxists and modern liberals have done. Scientism and philosophical materialism hides the spiritual reality of the individual.

At Fatima, Portugal, between 13 May and 13 October 1917, there occurred an extraordinary series of events—a tremendous supernatural manifestation which included heavenly signs, physical healing, and prophecies. On 13 May 1917 three shepherd children saw the apparition of a woman, said to be the Virgin Mary. Larger and larger crowds gathered in subsequent months. By October the numbers reached between 30,000 and 100,000 persons. The scientist, Jacques Vallee, described the Fatima event in terms of "luminous spheres, lights with strange colors, a feeling of 'heat waves,' all physical characteristics commonly associated with UFOs."[70] After thirteen years of careful investigation, the Catholic Church determined that the...

> solar phenomenon of the 13th of October 1917, described in the press of the time, was most marvelous and caused the greatest impression on those who had the happiness of witnessing it....
>
> This phenomenon, which no astronomical observatory registered and which therefore was not natural, was witnessed by persons of all categories and of all social classes, believers and unbelievers, journalists of the principal Portuguese newspapers and even by persons some miles away. Facts which annul any explanation of collective illusion.[71]

The shepherd children at Fatima were shown "a great sea of fire which seemed to be under the earth. Plunged in this fire were demons and souls in human form, like transparent burning embers, all blackened…."[72] A prophecy was given to the children. The end of the First World War was foretold. If people "do not stop offending God another and worse one will begin during the reign of Pius XI." The apparition asked for the consecration of Russia "and the communion of reparation on the First Saturdays." The supernatural visitant reportedly stated,

> If my requests are heeded, Russia will be converted, and there will be peace; if not, she will spread her errors throughout the world, causing wars and persecutions of the Church. The good will be martyred; the Holy Father will have much to suffer; various nations will be annihilated. In the end, my Immaculate Heart will triumph. The Holy Father will consecrate Russia to me, and she shall be converted, and a period of peace will be granted to the world.[73]

For the unbeliever this sort of thing is not easy to accept, and Jacques Vallee (as a scientist) dismissed this prophecy as "a mixture of seriousness and absurdity" commonly associated with such phenomena. Many years later Vallee would adjust his position. "The word absurd," he admitted, "is misleading; I [now] prefer the expression *metalogical*."[74] According to Vallee the statements of interdimensional beings are "not simply absurd." There is, within such statements, symbolic meanings and associations. Here is a consciousness that transcends time and therefore must communicate through metaphor and *metalogic*.

> Situations such as these often have the deep poetic and paradoxical quality of … religious tales … and the mystical expressions of the Cabala, such as references to a 'dark flame.' If you strive to convey a truth that lies beyond the semantic level made possible by your audience's language, you must construct apparent contradictions in terms of ordinary meaning.[75]

In the case of the Fatima prophecy, however, when we consider the threat of nuclear war and Russia's errors spreading throughout the world, there is nothing absurd or illogical about various nations being annihilated. In truth, what statement about Russia, made a few weeks prior to the Bolshevik Revolution, could have been more prescient? It is only if we look through the temporal eye of the moment, which assumes the "end of the Cold War," that this sacred message appears "absurd." From the point of view of eternity, from the spiritual perspective, it is *our* secular utopia that must prove absurd.

In terms of our understanding, we ought to seek higher ground; that is to say, *spiritual* ground. Only then can we find the way ahead, as intended by our Creator, in accordance with those spiritual realities which underlie our physical world. Today's materialist rebellion readily denies all this. The revolutionary Marxists and their kindred have turned a deaf ear to the *metalogic* of divinity. They have not only captured our universities, they have poisoned our seminaries. They have brought their materialism and cynicism into the Church itself. By intentionally sowing moral confusion and error, by advancing a destructive credo, they have wrought perversion on every side. They have turned humanity against itself, in the name of humanity. Their confusions are many. Their utopian projects will fail, and various nations will be destroyed.[76] This is perhaps the intention, after all. There are those who are filled with hate instead of love, who are filled with enmity instead of friendship, and they have politically organized themselves.

Civilization has been built up gradually over the course of many generations. It is something specific, with its own unique origins and history arising out of a grand procession of spirit. This procession is a mystery. It is the impertinence and hubris of our politically organized rationalists to demystify and explain this procession. This demystification has been, from first to last, an exercise in self-deception. The ruling strata of civilization, having been conditioned to this rationalism, is now so thoroughly self-deceived that it has infected the whole of society with false perspectives, false expectations and values incompatible with man's real needs.

At the core of this regime of self-deception we find the notion that man is an abstract being who does not require a tribal or national identity—a being with no real occasion for enmity. But there is no such being. The real man of flesh and blood is not an abstraction. The ideologies of universal peace and prosperity being untrue, the political practices of the self-deceived must end in catastrophe. Therefore the cause of universal brotherhood now signifies the most violent epoch of all. Here the fool will be re-introduced to his enemy. Self-deception being exhausted, a terrible war must begin. From this we will regain our clarity. However great the destruction, society will recover. A new civilization will be built on the ruins of the old.

THE END

ENDNOTES

1 Carl Schmitt, *The Concept of the Political* (Chicago: University of Chicago Press, 2007), p. 26.

2 Edward Gibbon, *The Decline and Fall of the Roman Empire* (New York: Random House, The Modern Library), p. 102.

3 Gustave Le Bon, *The Man and His Works* (Indianapolis: Liberty Press, 1979), p. 85.

4 Genesis 11:6.

5 Ion Mihai Pacepa and Ronald Rychlak, *Disinformation: Former Spy Chief Reveals Strategies for Undermining Freedom, Attacking Religion, and Promoting Terrorism* (Washington, D.C., WDN Books, 2013), p. 38.

6 Jean Davidson, "UCI Scientists Told Moscow's Aim Is to Deprive U.S. of Foe," *Los Angeles Times*, 12 December. 1988. http://articles.latimes.com/1988-12-12/local/me-14_1_uci-scientists. Arbatov is quoted as saying, "Our major secret weapon is to deprive you of an enemy."

7 Arbatov himself was the founder of that institute.

8 Eric Pace, "Harry Eckstein, 75, Professor Who Studied Political Culture," *New York Times*, 11 July 1999. http://www.nytimes.com/1999/07/11/us/harry-eckstein-75-professor-who-studied-political-culture.html. In 1988, at the time of Arbatov's visit, Eckstein headed the UCI Political Science Department.

9 Wikipedia.org, Rein Taagepera, https://en.wikipedia.org/wiki/Rein_Taagepera.

10 Davidson.

11 Letters to the Editor, *New York Times*, 8 December 1987.

12 Anatoliy Golitsyn, *New Lies for Old* (New York: Dodd, Mead & Company, 1984), see the chapter titled "The Final Phase."

13 T.S. Eliot, "The Hollow Men," 1925.

14 Quest for Peace, Georgi Arbatov. https://www.youtube.com/watch?v=T-cIkq9GUWtw.

15 Davidson.

16 *Ibid.*

17 "Russia prepares nuclear surprise for NATO," *Pravda*, 11 November 2014.

18 "Russia prepares nuclear surprise for NATO," *Pravda*, 11 November 2014.

19 *Davidson.*

20 "Russia takes complete advantage of castrated armed forces of the

West," *Pravda*, 13 November 2014. http://english.pravda.ru/russia/politics/13-11-2014/129021-russia_usa_nuclear_weapons-0/

21 John Cole, "TV Interview for BBC ('I like Mr. Gorbachev. We can do business together'), 17 December 1984, http://www.margaretthatcher.org/document/105592.

22 Anna Politkovskaya, *Putin's Russia* (London: The Harvill Press/Random House, 2004), p. 68. She writes, "Well, is the return of the secret police a coincidence?" On p. 82 she describes the present Russian system as "a model that puts Soviet ideology at the service of big-time private capital." Here she implies that this is by design. She shows how Russian capitalism was controlled throughout by the Soviet *nomenklatura*.

23 "Russia takes complete advantage of castrated armed forces of the West," *Pravda*, 13 November 2014. http://english.pravda.ru/russia/politics/13-11-2014/129021-russia_usa_nuclear_weapons-0/

24 Carl Jung,, *Aion: Researches Into the Phenomenology of the Self* (Princeton, New Jersey: Bollingen Foundation, Inc., 1979), trans. R.F.C. Hull,   p. 43

25 See a youth poem written by 19-year-old Karl Marx in 1837, titled *Human Pride*: "With disdain I will throw my gauntlet / Full in the face of the world / And see the collapse of this pygmy giant / Whose fall will not stifle my ardour. / Then will I wander godlike and victorious / Through the ruins of the world / And, giving my words an active force / I will feel equal to the Creator."

26 Webster's *New International Dictionary of the English Language*, Second Edition unabridged (Springfield, Mass.: G&C Merriam Company, 1943).

27 *Patres Conscripti*: Conscript Fathers, which signifies the Roman senate or any similar body of male leaders.

28 Attributed to Euripides: Ὅταν ὁ δαίμων ἀνδρὶ πορσύνῃ κακά, / τὸν νοῦν ἔβλαψε πρῶτον.

29 See Phillip E. Johnson, *Darwin on Trial*.

30 John Milton, *Paradise Lost*, lines 35-63

31 *Paradise Lost*, Lines 159-165

32 *Ibid*, lines 254-55.

33 *Ibid*, line 157.

34 *Ibid*, lines 261-63.

35 Friedrich Nietzsche, trans. R.J. Hollingdale, *Thus Spoke Zarathustra*, Part II, "The Child With the Mirror."

36 Marx, Preface to doctoral thesis, in Karl Marx: Selected Writings, 12-13.

37 J.F.C. Fuller, *Armament and History: A Study of the Influence of Armament on*

History from the Dawn of Classical Warfare to the Second World War (New York: Charles Scribner's Sons, 1945), p. xiv.

38 World War I—as described by U.S. President Woodrow Wilson.

39 Francis Fukuyama, *The End of History and the Last Man* (New York: Avon Book, 1992).

40 *Ibid*, p. 300.

41 Friedrich Nietzsche, *Thus Spoke Zarathustra*, "Zarathustra's Prologue," part 5.

42 Fukuyama, p. 301.

43 *Ibid*, p. 313.

44 *The Concept of the Political*, p. 52.

45 Carl Jung, *The Archetypes and the Collective Unconscious, Collected Works* Part 1 Volume 9, par. 217 (Princeton: Princeton University Press).

46 Proverbs 29:18.

47 A remark attributed to Sigmund Freud by Carl Jung. *Memories, Dreams and Reflections* (New York: Vintage Books, 1965), p. 150.

48 Machiavelli (trans. Bernard Crick), *The Discourses*, 56.

49 *Ibid*.

50 Carl Jung, Flying Saucers: A Modern Myth of Things Seen in the Sky (Princeton: Princeton University Press, 1978), par. 784.

51 Charon is the boatman to Hades.

52 *Ibid*, para. 699.

53 Whitley Strieber, *Communion: A True Story*, (New York: Avon Books), p. 58.

54 Karla Turner, *Into the Fringe*, p. 57.

55 *Ibid*, p. 61.

56 *Ibid*, p. 72.

57 Jacques Vallee, *Dimensions: A Casebook of Alien Contact* (USA: Ballantine Books Edition, May 1989), p. 248.

58 *Ibid*, p. 249.

59 Stephan A. Hoeller, *Jung and the Lost Gospels: Insights into the Dead Sea Scrolls and the Nag Hammadi Library* (Wheaton: Quest Books, 1989), 232.

60 Stephen B. Oates, *With Malice Toward None: The Life of Abraham Lincoln* (New York: Mentor, 1977), p. 463. Oates took the story from *Recollections of Lincoln*, written by Ward Hill Lamon, p. 115-118.

61 Carl Jung, *Synchronicity: An Acausal Connecting Principal* (Princeton: Princeton

University Press, 1973), p. 8, para. 824.

62 Schopenhauer, *Transscendente Spekulation uber die anscheinende Absichtlichkeit im Schicksale des Einzelnen* (1851) in Schopenhauer's *sammtliche Schriften in funf Banden*, vol 4, pp. 264-65.

63 *Ibid.*

64 This is not to say that world history lacks *indirect* metaphysical significance.

65 John A. Keel, *Why UFOs: Operation Trojan Horse* (USA: Manor Books, Inc., 1976), p. 200.

66 John A. Keel, *The Eighth Tower* (New York: E.P. Dutton & Co., Inc, 1975), p. 69.

67 John A. Keel, *Our Haunted Planet* (Lakeville, Minnesota: Galde Press, Inc., 2008), p. 195.

68 Arthur Schopenhauer (trans. R.J. Hollingdale), *On the Indestructability of Our Being By Death*, section 5.

69 Mathew 4:4.

70 Jacques Vallee, *The Invisible College* (USA: E.P. Dutton, 1976), p. 142.

71 *Ibid*, as quoted by Vallee.

72 Santos, *Fatima in Lucia's Own Words* (2003), p. 123.

73 *Ibid*, p. 123-124.

74 *Dimensions*, p. 157.

75 *Ibid*, p. 158.

76 Consider the case of Venezuela.

Made in the USA
Las Vegas, NV
21 November 2020